Mind Hacking

2 Manuscripts Photographic Memory and Speed Reading

Logan G Davidson

© **Copyright 2018 by Logan G Davidson - All rights reserved.**

The following book is reproduced below with the goal of providing information that is as accurate and as reliable as possible. Regardless, purchasing this eBook be consent to the fact that both the publisher and the author of this book are in no way experts on the topics discussed within, and that any recommendations or suggestions made herein are for entertainment purposes only. Professionals should be consulted as needed before undertaking any of the action endorsed herein.

This declaration is deemed fair and valid by both the American Bar Association and the Committee of Publishers Association and is legally binding throughout the United States.

Furthermore, the transmission, duplication or reproduction of any of the following work, including precise information, will be considered an illegal act, irrespective of whether it is done electronically or in print. The legality extends to creating a secondary or tertiary copy of the work or a recorded copy and is only allowed with an expressed written consent of the Publisher. All additional rights are reserved.

The information in the following pages is broadly considered to be a truthful and accurate account of facts, and as such any inattention, use or misuse of the information in question by the reader will render any resulting actions solely under their purview. There are no scenarios in which the publisher or the original author of this work can be in any fashion deemed liable for any hardship or damages that may befall them after undertaking information described herein.

Additionally, the information found on the following pages is intended for informational purposes only and should thus be considered, universal. As befitting its nature, the information presented is without assurance regarding its continued validity or interim quality. Trademarks that mentioned are done without written consent and can in no way be considered an endorsement from the trademark holder.

Your Free Gift

As a way of saying thank you for your purchase, I wanted to offer you a free bonus E-book called **5 Incredible Hypnotic Words To Influence Anyone**

Download the free guide here: https://www.subscribepage.com/b1b5i8

If your trying to persuade or influence other people then words are the most important tool you have to master.

As Humans we interact with words, we shape the way we think through words, we express ourselves through words. Words evoke feelings and have the ability to talk to the lister's subconscious.

In this free guide, you'll discover 5 insanely effective words that you can easily use to start hypnotizing anyone in conversation.

Listen to this book for free

Do you want to be able to listen to this book whenever you want? Maybe whilst driving to work or running errands. It can be difficult nowadays to sit down and listen to a book. So I am really excited to let you know that this book is available in audio format. What's great is you can get this book for FREE as part of a 30-day audible trial. Thereafter if you don't want to stay an Audible member you can cancel, but keep the book.

Benefits of signing up to audible:
- After the trial, you get 1 free audiobook and 2 free audio originals each month
- Can roll over any unused credits
- Choose from over 425,000 + titles
- Listen anywhere with the Audible app and across multiple devices
- Keep your audiobooks forever, even if you cancel your membership

Click below to get started
Audible US - https://tinyurl.com/yxc32f5x
Audible UK - https://tinyurl.com/y4ysd7e2
Audible FR - https://tinyurl.com/yxdnn9r6
Audible DE - https://tinyurl.com/y538mwvw

Table of Contents

Photographic Memory 1

Introduction 3

Chapter 1: The Basics of Photographic Memory 7

Chapter 2: How Memory Works 17

Chapter 3: Debunking Photographic Memory Myths 27

Chapter 4: Unknown Facts about Photographic Memory 37

Chapter 5: Benefits of Developing a Photographic Memory 41

Chapter 6: Developing Memory for Revision Reading 51

Chapter 7: Strategies to Strengthen Photographic Memory 55

Chapter 8: Lifestyle Changes to Improve Your Memory 73

Chapter 9: Tricks to Improve Your Memory 81

Chapter 10: The Life of Those That Possess Amazing Memories 91

Conclusion 103

Speed Reading 105

Introduction..107

Chapter 1: Ways to Eliminate Your Bad Reading Habits..................................109

Chapter 2: Skimming and Scanning Material...123

Chapter 3: Reading Words in Groups....135

Chapter 4: Painting the Words...............145

Chapter 5: Pacer Techniques to Improve Speed Reading 155

Chapter 6: In-Depth Speed Reading......169

Chapter 7: Advancing Your Speed Reading Skills..183

Conclusion 195

Photographic Memory

Advanced Techniques to Improve Memory, Have Unlimited Memory and Accelerated Learning with Memory Techniques

Logan G Davidson

Table of Contents

Introduction 3

Chapter 1: The Basics of Photographic Memory 7

Chapter 2: How Memory Works 17

Chapter 3: Debunking Photographic Memory Myths 27

Chapter 4: Unknown Facts about Photographic Memory 37

Chapter 5: Benefits of Developing a Photographic Memory 41

Chapter 6: Developing Memory for Revision Reading 51

Chapter 7: Strategies to Strengthen Photographic Memory 55

Chapter 8: Lifestyle Changes to Improve Your Memory 73

Chapter 9: Tricks to Improve Your Memory 81

Chapter 10: The Life of Those That Possess Amazing Memories 91

Conclusion 103

Introduction

Welcome and thank you for purchasing *Photographic Memory* to hone your brain's unused skill sets!

It's 2 AM on a Wednesday night, and you're still studying. You are on your third mug of tea, your eyes are starting to blur, and no matter *what* you do you just can't get the stuff you need to know for that test tomorrow morning to stick. Wouldn't it be nice if you had a photographic memory? Then all you would have to do is read everything once. On the day of the test, you would be able to mentally pull up the page the important stuff was on, and like magic, all the info you need would be there. You would ace that test and ride off into the sunset.

Okay, I love metaphors, but the point is that the phrase photographic memory sounds a little bit like a magician's trick or a Hollywood cliché, well, because it is. Pop culture from celebrities to movies have used photographic memory to spice up storylines for years, but no one truly has it. When we talk about photographic memory, we

Photographic Memory

refer to those who can look at something, take a mental snapshot, and later remember every single detail perfectly. That snapshot might be so good that the person notices something they didn't see before. The thing is, *no one* has *this kind* of memory.

However, there are multitudes of ways that you can strengthen your brainpower to help you with those overwhelming tests, to remember details of recent events, and much more! There are techniques, tricks, and methods that you can use to harness your brain's power and use it to your advantage in many aspects of life.

In this book, you are going to discover:

- All the basics you need to know to understand what photographic memory is;

- How this kind of memory works;

- All the disbeliefs that surround the topic;

- The benefits of honing a better memory;

- How to develop a better memory with revision reading;

Chapter 1: The Basics of Photographic Memory

Tesla

This man had no issue reciting entire books, but also stated that he encountered very random and blinding depictions of light that were paired with hallucinations. He had the capability to go back in time within his mind, recalling distinct details of very early portions of his childhood.

Photographic memory is a blessing in disguise. Being able to recall numbers, words, names and other images and information with accuracy is quite a skill. These types of abilities are caused by the process of neuroplasticity within our brain, which provides us the capability of creating new connections by the breaking down of old ones.

Some people are naturally born with these abilities, while many others must practice and use particular techniques to sharpen their memories. The remaining chapters of this book will cover, in detail, some great tips and other vital information you need to know to get yourself on the right track; perhaps to someday remember this entire book!

Photographic Memory

"Everyone has a photographic memory, some just don't have film."

This quote is very true when it comes to understanding those who exhibit photographic memory. While research has been unable to find much valuable information or resources to verifying this way of remembering, there are certainly plenty of people ready to vouch for its certainty.

Chapter 2:
How Memory Works

Memory helps make us who we are, whether recognizing loved ones, recalling past joys, or just remembering how to walk and talk and fry an egg. Memory is the chain that connects our past to our present; if it breaks, we are left untethered and incapable of either leaving the present moment or embrace the future.

Memory isn't an all-or-nothing thing. Some memories can be processed automatically, and they are stored differently than your personal or factual memories, such as your first kiss or how to recite math equations or who won the Cold War.

Technically speaking, memory is learning that has persisted over time. It is information that has been stored and can be recalled. During situations like remembering information during an exam, our brains' recollection system works in 3 different ways: through recall, recognition, and relearning. If you think back to all the kinds of tests you have taken during school, they're all designed to evaluate how you access stored information in these ways.

Recall is how you reach back into your mind and bring up information, just as you do on fill in the blanks on a test. So, if I say _____ is the capital of Greece, your brain hopefully will recall that the answer is Athens.

Recognition is more like a multiple-choice test. You only need to identify old information when presented with it, such as:

- Which of the following was not an ancient city in Greece?

  - Athens

  - Marathon

  - *Pompeii*

  - Sparta

Relearning is sort of like refreshing or reinforcing old information. When you study for a final exam, you relearn things you half-

Chapter 2: How Memory Works

forgotten more easily than you did when you were first learning them, such as a basic timeline of the Greek Empire.

The stages of storing information

But *how?* How does all that data that were exposed to all the time every day become memory? In the late 1960s, American psychologists Richard Atkinson and Richard Shiffrin figured out the basics of memory enough to break it into three stages:

First, it is *encoded* into the brain, then *stored* for future use and then eventually *retrieved*. Sounds simple, right? By now, you may have figured out that just because you take a lot of stuff about your mind for granted doesn't mean that it is not complicated.

Atkinson and Shiffrin's model refers to recording things we want to remember as an immediate but fleeting sensory memory. If you do recall something after seeing it for just a few seconds, it's because you successfully managed to shuffle it into your short-term memory where you probably encoded it through rehearsal. This is how you briefly remember things like phone numbers and passwords.

Photographic Memory

However, this information only stays in your short-term memory for under 30 seconds without a lot of rehearsal. Unless you repeat those small chunks of information repeatedly, you are likely to forget it quickly since your mind, amazing as it is, can only store 4 to 7 distinct bits of information at a time, to where it gets erased or stored into long-term memory.

Long-term memory

Long-term memory is like a durable and ridiculously spacious storage unit, holding all your knowledge skills and experiences. Since the days of Atkinson and Shriffin, psychologists have recognized that the classical definition of short-term memory didn't capture all the processes involved in the transfer of information to your long-term memory.

Later generations of psychologists revisited the whole idea of short-term memory and updated it to the more comprehensive concept of *working memory*.

Working memory

Working memory involves *all* the ways that we take short-term information and stash it in our long-term stores. Increasingly we think of it as involving both explicit and implicit processes. Those ways are:

- Visual-spatial information
- Central executive
- Auditory rehearsal

Explicit memory

When we store information consciously and actively that's an explicit process. We make the most of this after the working memory when we study so that we can know that Athens is the capital of Greece, Pompeii was a Roman town and not a Greek one, for example.

We capture facts and knowledge that we think we're going to need. Like when you are told to remember something specific like a name or number, you concentrate on that detail and file it away, even if just for a brief time.

Implicit memory

We are not conscious of *everything* we take in, but our working memory often transfers stuff

Photographic Memory

we're not aware of to the long-term storage. We call this an implicit process, the kind you don't have to actively concentrate on.

A good example might be a classically conditioned association; if you get all sweaty and nervous at the dentist because you had a root canal last year. You don't *need* to pull up that file in your brain on the last time you got your face drilled down to think, "<u>Oh, oral surgery. NOT my favorite</u>." The implicit process covers all this automatically.

Automatic Processing

All types of automatic processing are hard to shut off. Unless you have something unusual going on in your brain, you might not have much choice but to learn this way. For instance, the way you learned to not put your hand into a fire. That learning would have happened automatically as soon as you first yank your hand away from an open flame.

Whether those things are locked explicitly or implicitly or both, they are different kinds of long-term memory.

Chapter 2: How Memory Works

Procedural Memory

Procedural memory refers to how we remember to do things, such as riding a bike or reading. It's difficult to learn at first but eventually, you can do without thinking about it.

Episodic memory

Long-term memory can also be episodic, tied to specific episodes in your life, such as remembering that time that Grace fell out of her chair in chemistry, and everybody started laughing uncontrollably.

There are other kinds of long-term memory too. We are continuously learning about the psychology of the whole complex phenomenon.

Tricks for Healthy Memory

For healthy memories, there are all sorts of tricks to help you improve your memory capabilities.

Mnemonics help with memorization, and I'm sure you know a few that take the form of acronyms, such as:

- ROY G. BIV for the colors of the rainbow

Mnemonics work, in part, by organizing items into familiar manageable units with a process called _chunking_. For example, it may be hard to recall a number with 7 digits, but it is much easier to commit to memory in the rhythm of a phone number.

Strategies like mnemonics and chunking can help you with explicit processes but _how_ well you retain your data can depend on how deep you dig through the different levels of processing.

Shallow processing

Shallow processing lets you encode information on basic auditory or visual levels based on the sound, structure, or appearance of a word.

Deep processing

To really retain information, you must activate your deep processing, which allows you to encode semantically based on actual meanings associated with the word.

If you really want to make information stick in your mind, you will want to connect it to something meaningful or related to your own personal emotional experience. How much

Chapter 2: How Memory Works

information you encode and remember depends on both the time you took to learn it and how you made it personally relevant to you.

Memory is extremely powerful. It's constantly shaping and reshaping your brain, your life, and your identity. Our memories either haunt us or sustain us, but either way, they define us. Without them, we are left to wander alone in the dark.

Chapter 3:
Debunking Photographic Memory Myths

The ultimate questions of photographic and eidetic memory have yet to be 100 percent proven by science, which makes it difficult to decipher if people truly possess these abilities or if they are just awesome at retaining information and memory more naturally than others. Because of this lack of proof, there are several myths around the idea of photographic memory, which we will be debunking in this chapter.

The Most Common Myths about Photographic Memory

Photographic memory works just like a camera

If only! You would be surprised at the number of people who truly think that this kind of memory works just like a camera; a simple 'click!' and you have captured information forever! Perhaps this can be a futuristic idea, but photographic memory, unfortunately, doesn't work this way.

The decline of remembering information occurs gradually

Forgetting details of a piece of information or a specific event often happens right after it has occurred. If you fail to take those details away with you from that experience, that piece of information will be lost within your mind for eternity. Even those that possess aspects of a photographic memory don't have the power to remember things they choose to block out.

Confidence is an indicator of having a great memory

Naturally, when you can remember more information that the person beside you at the drop of a hat, you are going to get a nice stroke to your self-confidence. But confidence should not be the ultimate sign that someone has a great memory.

Chapter 3: Debunking Photographic Memory Myths

Events that are emotional result in accurate memories

Traumatic experiences can be revisited in the future in vivid details, but those memories can just as easily be eliminated from your mind as well. This goes for any type of event that you have endured that falls into the stressful category.

Negative memories can be buried and recovered later in life

Many people believe that negative memories can be repressed for some time and that they can be buried for eternity. It is also believed that even though memories may be buried, that they can be dug back up with the help of a psychologist or hypnotist. This myth depends on the individual.

Some wish to repress their memories, and others wish to unbury them to later cope and move forward with their lives. No matter what, people who have been abused mentally, physically or emotionally, will always have some recollection, no matter how much effort goes into deeply burying those memories.

Memory is a "thing"

Many folks think that their memory is an object that they can pick up, warp and mold to their liking. You cannot say that one part of your memories is "healthier" than others.

<u>Memory is a process</u> and should be viewed as an activity. Just like activities that you perform throughout everyday life, you may recall things in a good or bad fashion. Recalling things more easily takes practice and skill, "practice makes perfect."

Memories are only stored in one area of the human brain

False! There is not *one* place in the human brain that is responsible for storing all our recollections. Individual pieces of our memories are created from tiny fragments of memories that occur over time.

The memory process is built up of a complex integration of many different factors. All our memories are stored in various methods and placed within different areas of the brain. Even

Chapter 3: Debunking Photographic Memory Myths

similar kinds of memories are recalled in various ways.

There is a secret in becoming a master at recall

Sadly, there is no secret that critics are keeping on the topic of recollection. Different methods of improving your memory depend on what works best for the individual. There are lots of various memory skills to improve memorizing different types of information. Many of those methods have been around for as much as 2,000 years.

There is no quick way to improve your memory, but you can learn more about the way you learn and retain information by utilizing different kinds of methods. If one doesn't work well for you, try another! What do you have to lose?

There are "easy" ways to memorize

People who are looking to enhance their memorization skills look for the easy ticket to the train of expertise. They think by learning one trick they will then be able to master photographic memory. Those with this mindset end up very disappointed. *Memorization is a*

<u>*learned skill*</u>. There is no "easy" way to go about it. There are many variables that go into becoming a great driver. The same goes with acquiring memorizing skills, it requires some effort on your part to get the most out of it.

You are stuck with your negative memories forever

Picture memory as a cardboard box; Those with a good memory have a bigger box, and those with weaker memories have a smaller box. As we acquire a new skill set, it is written on a piece of paper. Those with the bigger box throw in the papers, while the one with a smaller box must take the time to place each piece of paper nice and neat inside their box.

Even though the person with the weaker natural memory has a smaller box, theirs is more organized, making it much easier to recall information. This entire box metaphor debunks this theory that you will be stuck with your bad memories.

Chapter 3: Debunking Photographic Memory Myths

Hypnosis can retrieve lost memories

It is heavily believed that everything we see and experience is stored deep inside our brain. We believe that there is a method to reach it, the idea of hypnosis being a popular one. Sadly, hypnosis rarely ever aids in proper recollection, but rather has the potential to harm our faith in memorization.

Having amnesia means you forget everything, including your identity

We have all seen at least one or more movies that suggest that those who suffer from amnesia have forgotten all their past life. Realistically, amnesia is caused by illness or damage to vital areas of the brain that make it sometimes impossible to collect and store new memories.

With certain degrees of amnesia, it is difficult, if not impossible, to create short-term memories from long-term ones. Those that suffer in real life can easily recall past stories but are never able to tell you what they wore, did or consumed that same day.

Photographic Memory

Some people possess natural photographic memories

It is unlikely that anyone has the memorization skill set of a robot. When people undergo memory tests, they are likely utilizing memory skills to recall information. People mistake photographic memories with the mere practice of memorization techniques. So, in other words, if you take the time to learn photographic skills, you too can be just as sharp as those that claim they do!

You only have a certain period to hone your memorization skills

You are *never* too old to learn! While it is true that the older you get, the more difficult it can be to remember, older people who utilize memory skills often can remember just as much as an average 20-year-old. No matter the age, a human being has quite the capability to learn and process information.

Chapter 3: Debunking Photographic Memory Myths

Memorizing things constantly helps to boost memory

Memorizing things repeatedly will not create a brain that is better able to memorize. If you practice memorizing skills instead of attempting to always memorize a certain set of information you will improve your overall memory. Period.

Those with trained memories never forget

Even if you dedicate yourself to practicing photographic memorization skills, it doesn't mean you will remember everything. An ironic aspect about the human brain is that it tends to remember things it *wants* to recall. No matter how many memorization skills you learn, you are going to still forget some things. However, you will be able to recall things much easier and clearer than you used to.

Memorizing too much clutters the mind

Think back to the box analogy we used earlier; recalling doesn't depend on how much information you can soak up and retain. It depends on how well you mentally organize the information you acquire.

That's why it is essential to keep the things you want to recall organized and easy to mentally find. The capacity that our brains have is boundless; the more we learn, the easier it is for our minds to retain that new incoming information.

Only 10% of the brain is utilized by most people

There is not a single way to measure brain power that scientists have agreed to use, meaning no one knows how much of the brain we use. However, it is true that many of us fail to use our brains to their fullest potential. This is why memory training and brain expanding activities are essential in keeping a healthy mind. By learning memory skills, we can boost our brain power and improve our memory if we decide to take the initiative to do such.

Chapter 4: Unknown Facts about Photographic Memory

Photographic memory has been used as an excuse

Those blessed with higher terms of memory retention have used their gift as an excuse when they have knowingly screwed up during writing assignments, plagiarizing content that they supposedly "memorized" and then used by accident.

Exceptional memory is seen many times with disabilities

Individuals with mental disabilities, such as Down's syndrome, have been shown to harness amazing memorization skills. If you remember the movie Rain Man, it was based on a real-life man named Kim Peek. It was said that he read and could recall every page of 9,000 different books he had read in his lifetime. This type of memory greatly surpasses a regular human being's mental capabilities when it comes to retaining that kind of information.

Good memories are good for a reason

Those that possess phenomenal memorization skills and techniques typically can only be that amazing at retaining and recalling information from just one subject area most of the time.

The more time you spend 'exercising' your brain, the better it performs

Our brains are just like muscles and can become 'buff' over time. The more time you take to mentally exercise your mind, the more connections you can form from cell to cell within your brain. The more connections there are, the more brain power you have to retain and later recall information.

Some memorization skills are gifts, while some take practice

Children who possess the abilities of an eidetic memory are naturally born with it. Some scholars exhibit phenomenal memory naturally,

Chapter 4: Unknown Facts about Photographic Memory

too. There is nothing others can do to acquire those abilities to the levels in which these special people have. But there are many who have great memorization thanks to their dedicated time and disciplined practice.

Eidetic memory is mostly found in children

Scientists are still unsure why there are more children than adults that have eidetic abilities. At about age six or seven, these capabilities begin to fade. This is due to childhood development. Our brains must be able to filter out unimportant information to function efficiently and effectively. Having all that data packed in our brains as a child who notices all sorts of details throughout their day can greatly hinder being able to have a functional and good working memorization.

Eidetic memory is not perfect

Even those that possess the ability to recall sequences of letters or numbers are never perfect 100 percent of the time. The accuracy greatly declines after a matter of just a few minutes.

Photographic Memory

There are mental abilities that mimic photographic memory

Those that claim that they have photographic memory perform in ways that mimic the greater aspects of this type of brain functioning. Some scholars can recall loads of information while teaching a class or writing a biography. Some people are skilled in the use of mnemonic devices. Other people really do have a good sense of an eidetic memory. But no one really has a profound photographic memory.

Chapter 5:
Benefits of Developing a Photographic Memory

Have you noticed that there are people in the world around you that are confident, intelligent, and successful? They likely have developed their photographic memory to an enhanced state. It doesn't mean that these people are more intelligent than we are, they just have a skill set that we have yet to master.

How is it that the successful people seem to have success in many aspects of their lives? When I was at school, there were students who would easily breeze through tests and didn't seem to have the stress of studying like the rest of us.

When I joined the workforce, there would be colleagues who would give presentations with ease and poise. These people were accurate, had great attention to detail, were organized and very thorough. They would also have meaningful relationships that thrived.

It's a fact that what sets these people apart is their ability to memorize and then recall large amounts of information with ease. Superior intellect is not necessarily what these folks possess, but an ability for photographic memory whether developed and learned or naturally given.

The neural pathways in the brain become stronger when you develop your photographic memory, which opens more parts of the brain that may not have been used much before. Developing photographic memory increases your overall brain activity and brings benefits to many areas of your life, such as:

- Increased reading speed and comprehension

- Increased peripheral vision and awareness

- Greatly improved concentration and focus

Chapter 5: Benefits of Developing a Photographic Memory

All these things enable one to learn so much faster and more effectively, but it does take practice and discipline.

Once I realized the benefits to be gained from having a photographic memory, my journey began to find how I could develop this type of almost super-human power. It is thought that all of us are born with a photographic memory, but as we grow older, our habits stop us from using this skill. We can develop it again, thankfully, and reap the benefits it has on our lives. There are now a few courses that you can take to develop your photographic memory. Some start with a speed reading, but photographic memory is so much more than just a speed reading ability.

Benefits of Improved Memory

Better judge of character

Being able to judge character, especially when you are meeting new people, is essential. It can help you to assess facial expressions and people's posture correctly, which can help you to decide if you should socialize with them or avoid them.

Photographic Memory

When you start off in a new place, you can figure out right away and have all that information on good character memorized to easily determine who you should add to your group of friends and who you should avoid.

Ability to study with ease

Imagine having a test tomorrow and not having studied a second for it? Frightening, right? When you have a developed photographic memory, all you have to do is look through your notes and textbook information, and you are free to go about your life.

Ability to remember a lot more information

With a well-defined memory, you are better able to remember tiny details, from what someone wore on a certain day to exact layouts of obstacles courses, etc.

You can recall small details

With a photographic memory, you can notice details that many other folks often overlook.

Chapter 5: Benefits of Developing a Photographic Memory

Improved organization

With a better memory, you are better able to organize physically and mentally, meaning you can organize your thoughts and pertinent information in such a way that you can recall them later with ease., You are also better able to remember where physical items are, etc.

You can master intricate activities

If you have ever observed painters, you will notice that they do quite a bit of staring when looking at the subject they are painting. This is because they are trying to take in all those tiny details and get them as precise as they can. Those with eidetic memory can create portraits with just a few glances at a stranger.

Other Benefits

Have you ever stopped to think what really sets people apart? Throughout school, there was always that one student in the class that seemed to breeze through the toughest tests, while you sat there, trying to recall the answer to a certain question. There are those that can perform presentations with only a few minutes of

Photographic Memory

preparation and some of us that take a week before the due date to just attempt to nail each word we wish to convey.

In the workplace, there are those that are almost always precise in their work, highly detailed and organized to a fault. These individuals also seemed to have the best relationships, remembering things about others that many of us would forget right after obtaining.

An important aspect of what sets people apart is their mere ability to memorize and recall with ease whatever they desire. These people are not necessarily superior to others with above-human powers, they simply possess photographic memory on different levels.

But what, in fact, is the point of taking the time to learn the ways of obtaining the amazing abilities of photographic memory? Within this chapter, you will gain insight into the many positives, as well as a few negatives, that inheriting photographic memory has to offer.

Chapter 5: Benefits of Developing a Photographic Memory

Stronger neural pathways

When you begin to develop enhanced memory, this opens up the doors to parts of your mind that you were not aware of before. There are many areas of our brains that never get used to their fullest potential, which is actually very unfortunate. Imagine what we could do if we all used every inch of our beautiful mind?

When you begin to really develop a better memory, you will notice:

- Increased activity in your brain that makes other aspects of your life better

- Faster reading speeds

- Ability to comprehend new information at a quick rate

- Improved concentration and focus

Able to recall small details with ease

When you create the capability to take in so much information all at once, you will consequently notice that you can recall details of experiences much better.

Cons of Improved Memory

Even the best things have a negative side to them:

Recalling things that you don't want to remember

Those with photographic memory recall and visualize things to the tiniest detail, even things they wish could otherwise be erased from their memory altogether. This includes things about people they may not even know personally but may have seen for only a matter of minutes.

Unable to control memories

There are some people who have the sort of memory that they are unable to control. For example, if one were sitting in math class learning a new lesson, they may remember every problem they acquired knowledge of previously regarding that same sort of lesson. This could tend to make one feel overwhelmed.

Chapter 5: Benefits of Developing a Photographic Memory

Recollections can take up tons of space in the brain

Just like the memory card of a camera eventually fills up and you have to delete some images to continue using it, our brains work the exact same way. Having hundreds of thousands of images and recollections of information flying around in your mind can cause it to become quite cluttered, which consumes a lot of mental energy and can create unnecessary stress, as well as a feeling of being overwhelmed.

Being misunderstood

Most people do not know and do not have a photographic memory, which means they are unable to relate to the way you view and absorb information. Some may even be alarmed by the way you can memorize certain things. If someone is staring at them to figure them out right off the bat, it is not a great ice-breaker at first, to say the least.

Recalling negative bad memories

Those with enhanced memory can recall precisely what their ex-significant other looked

Photographic Memory

like when they broke up with them. They can remember the faces of the entire class when they embarrassed themselves. They will recall bloody images from movies and childhood wounds they received as a child.

Chapter 6: Developing Memory for Revision Reading

Exams are coming...three very scary words, right? And nothing will stop you from acing your tests like THE FOG. You know the feeling; you have read the same page over and over but the facts just won't stick in your mind. There is page after page of mind numbing notes you must get through, but how can you fit it all in? Before it all gets too overwhelming, remember, you are not alone and there are very simple things you can do to improve your memory!

The Different Types of Learning

First you need to find out what kind of learner you are. You can do this by seeing what characteristics match your learning style the most or try out multiple choice tests online. You could very well be a mix of different types. Once you know, you can start tailoring your revision accordingly.

- **Visual learners** are those who learn visually and prefer to see information and visualize the relationships between ideas being presented.

    o Do the best with graphics and charts and with highly visual presentations where one can easily see the relationships between various points.

- **Auditory learners** are those that prefer to hear information rather than see, visualize, or read it.

    o Do best by reciting the information aloud to remember it later

    o Need a chance to repeat points of information back to themselves or others in the form of questions or asking other people questions.

Chapter 6: Developing Memory for Revision Reading

- Set facts and pertinent information to rhythms you can easily remember.

- **Reading and writing learners** are those that learn the best by reading and/or writing information. This allows them to interact with the text, which is more powerful for them to memorize than hearing or seeing images.

  - Do best with quizzes that provide them a chance to write down things they have learned.

  - They like annotated handouts of presentations so that they can read along with the information being taught.

- **Kinesthetic learners** are those that prefer hands-on and experimental learning. They learn the best when they are doing something.

  - Add exercises in with this type of learning so that they can move

> around and demonstrate information they have learned.
>
> o Get them to jot things down to remember them later as well.

All the above tips under each variation of learning will help you boost your memory's overall effectiveness. Those tips also help add meaning and context to what you're trying to learn. It's the restructuring and reorganizing that really makes you remember.

The good news? Once you started putting these techniques into practice, make sure to take a break. Resting after learning something new helps you remember it for longer! Exams might be coming, but guess what? You will be fine!

Chapter 7: Strategies to Strengthen Photographic Memory

Can you harness this human super-power for yourself? The answer is most often YES! You can easily learn how to remember more things in a clear frame of mind by just learning techniques and practicing them on a regular basis.

This chapter is full of unique strategies for those that struggle with retaining information to help learn the secrets of this skill, as well as tips and tricks for those that wish to further enhance their memory skills. Within this chapter, there are going to be several different techniques provided for beginners to experts.

Before we look at these strategies to a sharper mind, it is important to remember some of the fundamentals of what makes up memory itself:

- We remember things that stand out to us, things that are offensive, sexually driven, funny, or plain absurd.

- We are exceptional at recalling dimensional information, routes, and layouts.

- Our minds are naturally visual creatures, and it is the most common way we learn and retain information from the outside world.

The Memory Palace

If we look back in history, this method of memory enhancement was used by many of our ancestors starting in the 5th century. The term 'palace' plays a pertinent role in this method, so pay attention.

Are you going to need to remember those lecture notes to give that amazing speech in a few days? You can do it! View your memory as a hard drive that stores everything you have absorbed in your lifetime so far. Our brains are great at remembering some things but terrible at recalling others. It does not take much in any of

Chapter 7: Strategies to Strengthen Photographic Memory

the following methods in this chapter to get frustrated. The trick is, however, to work *with* your memory. When you get frustrated, you will work against it, which will leave you wandering for hours, never being able to recall those words that will capture your audience's attention.

Our great ancestors did not have to recall long lists but rather needed to recall things to survive. We thrived on hunting and gathering. Even though we did not need to memorize numbers or instructions, we still needed to remember where to search for food, and the quickest way to our shelters, as well as what plants not to eat and which foods provided the best nutrients.

It was from then on that we gradually became better and more apt to remembering less vital things through the means of visuals and spatial information. You are not alone if you struggle to recall your grocery list or phone numbers. Humans are not mentally graceful this way, but we are when it comes to remembering places. This is where the title of this technique comes in!

Memory experts have learned to not work against the brains' natural rhythms, but instead, work with them to set-up easy to recall formats. It is all about taking the memories we struggle to recall and turning them into the types of memories that our brains are equipped to handle. Remember those fundamentals mentioned previously? Here are the steps to mix them together to help you recall any kind of information!

Step One: Build your palace

Think of a building that you know the layout of rather well, such as your childhood home. This is a great place to start with this exercise because it is seared into your mind with intimate detail, which gives you more power to build it.

Step Two: Create images

Do you want to learn to better memorize your grocery list? Then create items to later store in your palace that coincide with your list. Remember to use your imagination! The more funny or bizarre, the easier it will be to recall them. Unbelievably the course of evolution itself has hardwired the topics of jokes and sex into our core thinking, which is why many people

Chapter 7: Strategies to Strengthen Photographic Memory

associate items they need to remember into these two categories the most.

Step 3: Place imagery into your palace

Going back to the grocery list analogy, walk through your childhood household in your mind and place the memorable objects within the house in the order that you need them to be in. If done correctly, you should only have to retrace your steps one to two times to recall what you need to get from the store.

Step 4: Take a stroll in your palace

Once your items are in your mental palace, it is time to take a walk through it to ensure that can recall everything. This strategy does not only have to be used for simple things such as a grocery list. Many lecturers use it to connect points within their speeches. Yes, with this method your mind is going to be filled with a variety of things, from human and animal parts to dinosaurs to other absurdities. Make it fun!

Photographic Memory

Memory palace example

- *You head into your house and once through the threshold of your front door, you view a cow on fire standing in your entryway. This symbolizes that you need to purchase burgers at the store.*

- *Heading through the hallway, you see that your stairs are wet with the cow's blood. This symbolizes that you need to get ketchup as well.*

- *Once at the top of the stairs, you see large human buttocks, symbolizing that you need to pick up hamburger buns.*

Mind Mapping Process

The process of mind mapping is all about the gathering of your thoughts in a visual format. This helps to ensure that you can embrace things with much more creativity as well as effectiveness. These maps are diagrams that connect you to the information you need to acquire and recall at a later time, whether it is learning about a new topic or obtaining a new skill set. Many professionals use mind mapping

Chapter 7: Strategies to Strengthen Photographic Memory

to expand their creativity, as well as to connect with others through the means of natural association, which leads to the generation of innovative new ideas faster.

No matter how many notes you take on a subject that you wish to learn about, mind mapping triumphs every time. They can help us see the bigger picture, which makes it easier to grasp and understand it more deeply. They have been proven to assist those to be more efficient, thanks to their ability to quickly judge complex projects much easier. The best part? As new ideas are spun, new paths can be explored! There is no "basic" way to create a mind map. Whether you use pen and paper or embrace technology if it leads you to the right path that is what matters. Just remember to be creative!

Photographic Memory Training Tips

Training to sharpen your memory skills is quite simple. In fact, even a child can learn some of these techniques without too much hassle or effort. These tips will not only help you improve your memory but will also help you be able to recall information at a much quicker rate.

Lessen distractions

Being able to minimize things that distract you is one of the best ways to develop a skill in recalling memory. Do not blame your forgetfulness on memory, but rather turn the blame to the distractions that plague us each day. Do your best to focus on one thing at a time, instead of trying to take on multiple things at once.

Improve your lifestyle

Many memory issues that we face are due to our body's response to anger, depression, anxiety, and other negative feelings. It is important, not only for your recall rate but also for your overall well-being, to keep symptoms that can negatively impact you physically, mentally, and emotionally at bay. Ensure that you spend plenty of time doing things that you love and learn from.

Get moving

Physical activity helps increase the flow of blood to every part of your body, including the brain. Exercise allows those essential nutrients along with more oxygen to reach our brains so that

Chapter 7: Strategies to Strengthen Photographic Memory

they can perform better! 30 minutes of exercise 5 days a week is plenty. But more is even better.

Activate your brain

Your brain should be considered a muscle; if you don't use it, you will eventually lose it. The more we use it, the better it will perform when we really need it to. Try to incorporate some of these brain-stimulating activities into your daily schedule to get your brain off autopilot and concentrating on something more invigorating:

- Learn a new language
- Learn how to play an instrument
- Perform crossword puzzles
- Play a board game
- Read the newspaper or a book

Visualization

Visualization can improve your memory retention. Ensure that you practice visualization techniques and use image associations on a regular basis.

Military techniques

There are vital tricks that our own military use while in the line of duty and in combat, such as psychic spying and objective viewing. They can remember coordinates, locations, and images with these techniques, which are essential not only for their survival but their mission and those they are with.

Courses and exercises

There are hundreds of courses and things you can do to improve your memory. This could be from picture games, telling stories, building lists, and word association exercises. These games make it seem like you are not even learning or practicing memory retention and are effective at getting the job done.

Become self-directed

You are the only one that can take control of what you get out of the knowledge you acquire. Ask questions if needed! There are plenty of

Chapter 7: Strategies to Strengthen Photographic Memory

ways to obtain resources to receive the help you need! The more you inquire, the faster you learn things.

Build your background knowledge

When we take the time and initiative to learn things on our own accord, the more quality of learning improves in the long run.

Create discipline in learning

When you go into your sessions of memory training, you need to go in with a mind clear of all other distractions. Easier said than done, I know. Multi-tasking, no matter how beneficial our society claims it is, is not to be done while undergoing memory sessions. This also means while you are putting your learning curves into practice in real life as well. If your mind is preoccupied, this leaves very little room to conduct a photographic memory session completely. Do not divide up your attention into various sections. Keep your attentive eye on that memorizing prize!

Photographic Memory

Decide your learning objectives

Whenever you finally get the spark to acquire any new knowledge, it is important to ask yourself why you want to learn this and if it is worth your time and energy. Determine your purpose of learning and practicing something. This way, you will pay better attention and give it more special recognition as you go along.

Memory Strategies

Use image associations

This tip especially comes in handy for attempting to locate something that you cannot find. If you are looking for a book or car keys, take a second to imagine where they would be. If you book is perhaps called "A Hundred Suns," visualize what a hundred of those suns would appear like. Imprinting images within your mind can help you recall the book and perhaps find it later too.

Repetition of names

If you are one that struggles with recalling people's names or names of certain things, you

Chapter 7: Strategies to Strengthen Photographic Memory

are not the only one. Many people have a hard time retaining names, especially when trying to remember more than one or two names at once.

- After meeting someone, repeat their name back to them. "It is so nice to meet you 'so-so.' If you did not hear their name correctly or didn't hear quite how they pronounced it, clarify it right then to avoid asking it again later, saving yourself from the embarrassment.

- Learn to associate newly acquired names with someone you already know with the same name. If you do not know someone personally by that name, think of characters in books or favorite films. This association assists with recalling the names at a later time.

Utilize 'chunking'

Even though this technique sounds more like an issue that your car is having, it is actually a psychological phrase about a memory retention process that involves the clumping together of items, words, numbers, etc. on the same list to ensure you remember them.

Photographic Memory

- If attempting to memorize your grocery list, put all items into categories, such as fruits, veggies, frozen, condiments, meats, etc. Or, you can even categorize lists by meals you are going to make from the items you are trying to memorize.

- Dividing sets of specific numbers into smaller sections will help you recall telephone, social security, credit card numbers, etc. Instead of trying to remember an entire sequence of numbers, divide them up into sections. For example, instead of 1234567890, memorize it as 123-456-7890. This will assist you in repeating it back to yourself to ensure the proper memorization of it.

Get out those UNO cards

Or any deck of cards, for that matter. Whichever deck suits your fancy! You will be utilizing them for a while, so choose wisely. Draw the top three cards and try to memorize those cards. Then place those three back into the deck at random and spread them out. From the spread-out deck, choose your three cards and put them in the

Chapter 7: Strategies to Strengthen Photographic Memory

same order that they were earlier. Perform this exercise with three cards for a week, five the next week, then continue to increase your card count each week. Do this until you have the capability to memorize the entire deck in one sitting.

Domino trick

With a box of dominos make a pattern out of 10 of them. Memorize that pattern. Each week thereafter add 10 more dominos to your pattern. Do so until you can use the entire box. This method takes a while!

Picture engraining

This method is one used by our military to learn names and recognize faces quickly. You must not miss a day, or you have to perform this exercise for another week. You will need:

- A piece of paper that contains a cut-out box the size of 1 paragraph
- A paragraph of words you choose
- A windowless room
- A small but bright light

- Head to your darkroom and set up your light, turn it on and proceed to set up your paragraph so that the hole of your box covers up everything but the paragraph you wish to memorize. Look at the paragraph in front of you for 5 minutes. Turn off the light while you are still staring at the page. Repeat this same process each day for a month or until you can recall the paragraph in its entirety without any mistakes. This process utilizes light to engrain the visual of what you want to memorize into your brain.

Honing your Eidetic Memory Capabilities

Since we have discussed many ways to develop your photographic memory skills, we might as well touch base about a technique you can use to better your eidetic memory skills as well!

Training your brain to memorize in eidetic ways is not complicated, but it must be exercised in three ways: ***speed, space, and quantity***.

Chapter 7: Strategies to Strengthen Photographic Memory

Speed

This technique was created to train the speed at which you perceive and remember what you have seen. The idea is to make the amount of time you need to memorize shorter and shorter.

- o Utilize a program on your computer that lets you view something for short periods of time. Show things for 10 seconds to start out. And decrease over time as you grasp the training. People who can memorize at great speeds usually just have to look at things for less than 100 ms to memorize a list of say, around 10 numbers.

Space

The goal of this technique is to exercise the brain to memorize things that are separated by just a space that is big yet small enough for your eyes to visualize and memorize in a single glance. The idea of the space exercise is to memorize things without eye movement.

- o Write down a phone number that you can read in a single eyeshot. Ensure that you are only using your peripheral vision. To really train utilizing this technique a computer program that shows things in a separated way in both height and width is best. Start with shorter distances, gradually working your way up to farther distances while taking in more information.

Quantity

The goal of this technique is to memorize and remember as much information as you possibly can.

- o Utilize a computer program that provides you with items to memorize and gradually increase the number of subjects while lessening the time you have to do so. If you do not wish to use a program, writing or typing out telephone numbers is another great way, adding more numbers as you decrease your memorization time.

Chapter 8:
Lifestyle Changes to Improve Your Memory

Back in the good old days of research, it was believed that your brain function peaked during early adulthood and then declined slowly over time, resulting in lapses of memory and experiencing brain fog from time to time throughout the retirement years.

These days, it is well-known that the modern way of life plays a role in our cognitive decline, which is why when we continually expose ourselves to a poor diet, lack of quality sleep, chemicals, toxins, and stress, we are much less likely to use our memory to its full capacity.

When we live a healthier lifestyle, we support our brain health and encourage the growth of neurons. The memory center of your brain, known as the hippocampus, can produce new cells throughout your lifetime, which is what gives your brain the tools it needs to hone your memory skills. These tools are based on the lifestyle you live, which is a great news since it means you can change your daily routine to improve your memory!

Eat better

The foods you consume and don't consume play a vital role in how good your memory is. Fresh vegetables and healthy fats are crucial as you avoid carbohydrates and excess sugars.

- Brainpower foods:

    o *Walnuts, cauliflower, broccoli, celery*, and *curry* have compounds and antioxidants that protect your brain's health and help to produce new cells.

    o *Garbanzo beans, crab, red meats, blueberries*, and *healthy fats* are amazing foods for better brain health.

You also should increase your intake of animal-based omega-3's and reduce your consumption

Chapter 8: Lifestyle Changes to Improve Your Memory

of damaged omega-6 fats that are in items such as vegetable oil.

Exercise

When you get moving, you are encouraging your brain to work at its optimum capacity since it stimulates the nerve cells throughout the body. That allows those cells to multiply, become stronger, and form connections that keep your body and brain from becoming damaged.

It has been proven that those who exercise regularly were able to quickly grow and expand their memory center in the brain by a couple of percent per year.

Quit multitasking

Now more than ever, many of us perform the action of multitasking in all aspects of life; from home, to work, to when we drive, while we eat, etc. The reality is, multitasking slows us down and we are more prone to making errors as we become more forgetful.

Studies have proven that you need at least 8 seconds to truly commit to a piece of information if you wish to place it in your memory. If you are talking on the phone, carrying groceries, putting down your car keys and reading all at once, you are unlikely to remember anything.

The opposite of multitasking is being mindful. This helps everyone to gain a focus that cannot become distracted. Those that practiced mindfulness were found to improve their reading comprehension and expanded their overall memories since they were having to deal with fewer distracting thoughts.

Get quality sleep

Sleep is an action no human being can avoid, for it enhances your memory and allows you to practice and further improve your performance when it comes to learning challenging skills. Each night of sleep should be at least 4 to 6 hours. Otherwise, you could be majorly impacting your ability to think clearly.

Neuroplasticity, the process of brain growth, is the foundation for the way your brain behaves; this controls behavior, memory, and learning, which is fundamental to everyday life. Plasticity can happen when your brain's neurons are

Chapter 8: Lifestyle Changes to Improve Your Memory

stimulated by experiences and information from the outside world. A lack of sleep can inhibit this from ever occurring.

Allow your brain to play

If you fail to challenge your brain with new information, it starts to deteriorate. When you give your brain an appropriate amount of stimulus, you play an essential role in reversing brain degeneration.

This is why 'brain games' are vital to your brain's health and thus your memory. There are websites and mobile applications that you can use in your free time, such as Luminosity.com or Brain HQ. When you sit down to play these games, dedicate at least 20 minutes to them but don't perform the same task for more than 5 to 7 minutes at a time.

Master new skills

When you get involved in meaningful activities that have a purpose, you are stimulating your entire neurological system, which counteracts the effects of stress and reduces the likelihood that you will develop dementia later in life. It also promotes a healthier well-being.

One of the essential factors when it comes to improving your overall brain function is to engage in brand new tasks. The tasks you get involved in need to hold some sort of importance to you or be interesting or meaningful to hold your attention.

Use mnemonic devices

As you have read previously, mnemonic devices can really come in handy when you are trying to do your best to remember pertinent information. They are tools to help you remember words and concepts and involve organizing them in a format that is easy to remember.

- Acronyms
- Chunking
- Rhymes
- Visualizations

Chapter 8: Lifestyle Changes to Improve Your Memory

Making all the above changes to your lifestyle and daily routine will help you to retain a better memory over time as you practice the techniques and tricks you learn throughout this book! Your body is your temple; if you wish to accomplish big things, you need to take care of it. It is your foundation to success in this life!

Chapter 9: Tricks to Improve Your Memory

In the age of advanced technology and the broad span of the internet, it can be easy to dismiss memorization that impresses as a skill that is useless. As you have read, however, having a great recall can give you the upper hand in many situations. This chapter will discuss some cool and fun tricks that you can use to further enhance your memory capabilities.

Clench your right hand when learning and your left hand to recall

Seems weird, but there have been several studies to show that this easy trick can greatly improve your short-term memory. When you are learning something new or retaining information you need to recall in the future, all you need to do is clench your right hand into a fist.

Later, when you need to recall what you absorbed earlier, squeeze your left hand into a fist. So far, studies have shown that this handy trick only seems to work its magic in those that are right-handed.

Coordinate new information with a smell

Smells are a proven trigger when it comes to remembering memories, even better than sound. It's application, however, can be a bit tricky to master. It is recommended to coordinate smells from the time you are trying to memorize to when it needs to be recalled.

- For instance, spray a bit of perfume on the back of your hand or on your wrist as you are reading and then use that same perfume during your presentation, speech, or test.

Coordinate postures

It has been shown that if you keep the same position or posture while you are absorbing information and when you recall it, that it is easier to reach those memories.

Chapter 9: Tricks to Improve Your Memory

- Study in one position, such as at an angle with your legs crossed and then remember the answer to a test in that position.

Chew gum

There are a couple of legitimate theories for why chewing gum enhances memory. One is that the act of chewing leads to an increase in your blood flow, which helps the brain stay active as you memorize. The other theory is that chewing gum is an associated action with memories, which makes it easier to gain access to recollections. Pick up a pack of gum before study time!

Use melody

We all know that it is much simpler to recite the lyrics of a song than the words of a boring essay, right? Well, this is where the power of melody comes in handy if you need to ace a test!

There have been many studies to prove that the efficacy of melodies helps with the learning process. It may seem like a ton of additional work, but it is not hard to piggyback melodies that you love as you memorize new information.

Photographic Memory

Avoid staying up all night to study

Sleep helps to improve your memory and repetition while taking in information in mass forms decreases even immediate memorability. Distributing practices, which means studying for short bursts of time and taking a break, has been proven to be a better method to memorize information than staying up all night the evening before a test to cram.

Your best bet is to not procrastinate until the last minute and study new concepts a little at a time over just a few minutes each day. Use flashcards and other learning apps that are convenient for you to assist!

Use meditation

Buddhists are truly onto something with the whole meditation ritual. Whether you believe it or not, meditating helps to enlighten people. Meditating 4 times each day for as little as 20 minutes helps to increase cognition by as much as 50 percent! Get your Buddha on!

Chapter 9: Tricks to Improve Your Memory

Exercise more

If you find that some of the above suggestions are too tedious for your liking, then you may appreciate a physical approach more. There is a distinct connection between those that exercise on a regular basis to improve cognitive functioning, which includes memory retention. If you are looking to study and lose weight, this is a win-win scenario!

Drink less alcohol

When you abuse alcohol for a long period of time, this can wreak havoc on your overall memory and the ability to retain new information. While a drink every now and then is perfectly fine, if you are drinking to oblivion several times a month, then it pays to drink a bit less.

Use associations

Many of the tricks that help to improve your memory are all centered around one concept, association. We have dealt with involuntary association, such as recalling a smell or sitting in a similar position. Now, let's talk about voluntary associations.

Photographic Memory

There are some very simplistic voluntary associations. When you are starting to learn a new language, a sweet trick to remember is to associate new words with a word it sounds like in the language you already know. You will find that this makes it much easier to remember new words!

Bundle memories together

Pattern recognition is a great trick when it comes to the recollection of information. If you are trying your best to recall numbers, bundling memories all into one is a great method. If you can group them up in a meaningful way, you will be better able to remember longer strings of numbers.

For example, phone numbers can be split it up into something like 45 80 90 18. You can remember that the year 1945 was when WWII ended, associate 80's with the 80 and 90's with the 90 and the year 1918 is the year that WWI ended. This is better known as 'chunking' of words.

Chapter 9: Tricks to Improve Your Memory

Jot it down

Writing can activate areas of the brain that are known to store most of our retained information, which is why writing things out makes it easier to recall at a later date. If there is something essential that you need to remember, write it down!

Making a physical note and bringing it with you reinforces that information, no matter what circumstance, such as your phone breaking, etc.

Talk it out

While you don't have to perform long monologues to yourself in front of the mirror (but do as you wish!), you are better able to remember things once they are said aloud. In fact, this has been shown to improve accuracy by as much as 15 percent. Talking to yourself has also been shown to make you a smarter human being, so why not turn it into an everyday habit? However, it may be best that you practice this ritual in solitude.

Be mindful

One of the easiest ways to improve your memory is to be more consciously present in your day to day life and pay closer attention to what is being said, taught, and/or shown to you to understand. When you allow your mind to daydream, you fail to form memories and will have issues retrieving that information later.

Visualization

Visualization has been discussed several times in this book so far because it is an amazing way to enhance your overall memory. When you can create images in your mind, you can anchor new information with a symbol, making it much easier to recall.

Use repetition

If you need to remember a certain piece of information, especially a chunk that you find yourself forgetting, then repeat it to yourself, over and over again. This works best for objects, people, and locations and causes the information to become implanted and engrained within your mind.

Chapter 9: Tricks to Improve Your Memory

Find the 'why'

When you totally understand the reason behind the information you are attempting to retain, your mind becomes more intrigued by it, which makes it easier to memorize and use later.

Chapter 10:
The Life of Those That Possess Amazing Memories

You may know somebody who can review recollections without a moment's notice, while then again others may have never known about this cerebrum-controlled superpower. For huge numbers of us, it can be very hard to get a handle on this for the lion's share of us don't tackle this ability to recollect things and occasions in the finest of detail. Since there is little science to move down the likelihood of photographic memory being something that a few people are normally conceived with, while others can endeavor to learn it, it is imperative that we step directly into the shoes of those that claim and have given entirely sufficient confirmation that they have this capacity to see the world in an exceptionally definite organization. This section is brimming with exposures from individuals who have had individual experiences with this territory of their mind, and how this capacity to keep up memory so well has influenced their lives.

There have been numerous endeavors to get portrayals from those that say they can review things at a photographic rate. It is very intriguing to look at each piece of data that individuals can review with no issues. Some can clearly recollect the way something looks or the hints of a specific circumstance while others recall correct discussions verbatim. From the chateaus of a portion of the wealthiest individuals on the planet to those that abide in the filthiest regions of the greatest to littlest urban areas, the enchanted viewpoints that photographic memory brings to the table live in numerous spots here on our planet and in numerous places that we don't anticipate.

The Story of Betty

Betty, who dwells in west Michigan, claims she can imagine individuals, even those that she has looked at for seconds, in strong detail. She can recall subtle elements of the adornments they were wearing, down to what number of pearls or gems. She can review correct haircuts and how

Chapter 10: The Life of Those That Possess Amazing Memories

that specific individual did their make-up that day. She says that out of around eighty to one-hundred individuals she sees once a day between her drive to work and amid her work day, she can review eye-shading and diverse arrangements of garments every one of them tends to wear frequently, and points of interest of tattoos and a few discussions.

While reviewing harder to achieve circumstances in her brain, Betty can really envision herself walking around the scene at which that particular memory occurred. She asserts that it seems as though she sees the world she has officially gathered already from a birds-eye view. Indeed, even encounters and scenes that she dwelled in long, long ago can be gone by if she wishes. She says she discovered comfort in the review school play area back when she was a child, for her youth at home was not all that awesome.

Betty likewise expresses that she can tune in to music without the requirement for a radio, CD player or some other melodic gadget, for she can hear it by memory. The thing is, it now and then makes her crazy to review music along these lines since her psyche plays just a single instrument at any given moment.

Despite the considerable number of advantages that accompany having this apparently unnatural human "superpower", Betty says there are a couple of drawbacks, at any rate from her very own outlook. She cannot control when she envisions recollections. When she hears a specific piece of a specific tune, it triggers her psyche to go into a kind of time twist and influences her to return to the recollections her mind partners with that segment of the melody. Furthermore, with regards to figuring up math conditions or anything including numbers she is in for a psychological. When she is learning new conditions progressively, it triggers her brain to need to imagine different mixes of past lessons. This can make for a hard time focusing on nailing the exercise she is attempting to learn right now.

Even though it sounds astounding to have the capacity to flawlessly review extraordinary and agreeable encounters that she went through with others, it once in a while harms her when cherished one that she imparted those

Chapter 10: The Life of Those That Possess Amazing Memories

encounters to can't review them at all or not close as unmistakably as possible.

How is it for Betty to rest a few evenings? Awful, as she states. There are a few occasions where while she is trying to rest, terrible recollections will fly into her head, making a domino impact over her whole night's rest. She revealed when she sees or hears the voice of Winnie the Pooh, her mind naturally returns to a bad dream that she had when she was a child when the agreeable bear woke up and assaulted her violently.

Just a couple of individuals in Betty's own life think about her psychological capacities with regards to her memory maintenance. What's more, for those that know about her memory capacity, she gets asked: "Why are you not getting extraordinary evaluations on the off chance that you can recollect everything?" Her answer? Photos inside her memory are very divided, making it relatively difficult to assemble while she is trying or reviewing anything. It takes a ton of vitality to really envision one specific memory. She wishes she had significantly more control over her stunning mental and remembering abilities.

Photographic Memory

The Story of Jill

While a few people may have a light bulb moment when it comes to their capacity to recall, Jill's story is very novel. At the midlife age of her mid-forties, Jill Price is one of the most normally reported people who has expressed and demonstrated her psychological limit with regards to her photographic memory. She has been known as the 'lady who can't overlook.' Wherever she ventures, if there is something inside her surroundings that helps her to remember any kind of life circumstance she has already experienced, she tends to recount an anecdote about those past circumstances with whomever she is with at the time. Ms. Price has been recorded experiencing a one-on-one meeting with the prestigious Diane Sawyer about her memory capacities, that later was shown on the well-known television show, o 20/20. While on air Sawyer solicited Price to review minutes from TV history. She addressed each inquiry with exactness and on the ones that she couldn't review correct, point by point data, she could depict what she was wearing, eating, doing or the climate outside that specific day.

Chapter 10: The Life of Those That Possess Amazing Memories

Until her presentation on 20/20, numerous individuals had not known about Jill Price. Other than her nearby family and companions that were always amazed by her capacity to recollect everything with such exactness, the world was unaware of her. As per Price, while her grand memory framework was exceptional to others, it was sometimes a weight to her, and she needed answers in the matter of how and why her cerebrum worked not quite the same as everybody around her. In June of the year 2000, Price went over a site for a UC Irvine neuroscientist, James McGaugh and sent him a definite email, clarifying her circumstance. To her incredulity, he replied with some distrust. After meeting McGaugh's state of mind toward Price changed rather quickly, as he ran lab work and tests. He knew she was something exceptional. He acquainted Price with his group of specialists, who talked with her over the span of a five-years. The meetings were kept secret until the point that both Price and her new fan club were comfortable telling the general population. In 2006, an article composed by the associates highlighting Price was distributed in the Neurocase diary.

Photographic Memory

When this article was published, Price got offers from the media including Morning Edition. The day she was interviewed by Diane Sawyer for 20/20 the interview was taped for the following day's show of Good Morning America.

Prices' story, regardless of numerous faultfinders along her ride to the popularity she has gotten, is famously genuine. She has amazed a lot of people in her and has since spread her story to others, particularly the parts in which she has battled with her capacity. "There is a great deal of drawbacks with regards to keeping everything composed in my mind and reviewing it to others. Some days are dim and forlorn. There are days where I solidify up and can't review a solitary memory from my whole lifetime. Thank heavens that only keep going a couple of minutes. There are some days that I am anxious about the possibility that I will lose my great blessing for eternity. Also, there are some days I feel objectified for science and has a diversion for others. My experience turning out about my psychological capacities beyond any doubt has given me understanding with respect to how to appropriately deal with my blessing, and who acknowledges me for me". Since Price, nobody

Chapter 10: The Life of Those That Possess Amazing Memories

has come across anyone else with her valuable photographic memory abilities.

The Story of Andy

Much the same as each person on the planet, every one of us is exceptionally extraordinary in our own way. The same goes for how our brains hold and in the end review data. Andy's story is comparable to Betty and Jill's. He claims to have a remarkable memory, however just specific regions, particularly those with respect to examples and courses. He expresses that he can review examples and requests of things like groupings of numbers and word phrases. This goes for certain symbolism too. He additionally says that he can without a doubt recall specifics with overwhelming point of interest, portraying things down to the column of a sweater in which a string was adrift.

In Andy's school, he is notable for remembering expansive talks for class and discussing dates and conditions. At whatever point his t companions go on long excursions, they never bring along the GPS if Andy has been to those

Photographic Memory

spots since he can review road signs and recall correct turns.

Even though Andy likes his normal blessing, he needs to get a couple of things clear to those that are interested in how the psyches of individuals with incredible memory abilities work. Above all else, having higher memory maintenance does not make those individuals smarter than those with normal capacities with regards to memory. Despite the fact that they can recollect essential things for critical occasions, this does not mean they fundamentally comprehend what they have retained or recalled. For Andy specifically, remembering blends of numbers and letters is truly something he does to translate math conditions, entangled discourses, and different readings. He feels that his method for absorbing data is not the same as different children his age. He has figured out how to legitimately store every one of the parts of the data he obtains in the correct spots to filter through them at a later time.

He alludes to his capacity to remember things as a non-advanced rendition of a document framework. Despite the fact that Andy can

Chapter 10: The Life of Those That Possess Amazing Memories

inform somebody regarding a specific timeframe in relatively correct detail, if asked, this does not mean he can do so immediately without fail. "The data is there, it just sets aside some opportunity to recover it. It resembles some other normal human cerebrum, yet it is about how you store and sort out all the data we get on an everyday premise." Andy says that if a specific date was more critical to him, more subtle elements emerge to him more rapidly than unexceptional days where his mind did not feel the need to retain everything in his environment.

"Indeed, even those like me need to recollect that we are just as human and that regardless of how hard we attempt to hold everything, we are as yet going to overlook a few things."

As an understudy, Andy has taken in the most difficult way possible that liquor incredibly restrains his capacity to recall occasions and review things that he took in the night prior to a major gathering over an end of the week. He tells individuals that anybody can practice their cerebrum, it is about the amount you truly need to learn in a lifetime.

Conclusion

I want to congratulate you on making it to the end of *Photographic Memory*! Now, it is time for a quiz!

Just kidding, no quiz today, but once you begin to learn and harness the power of the memory-enhancing strategies in this book, perhaps I will have a test for you to conquer by then!

As you have learned, photographic memory may not be as possible as it is for those in the Hollywood movies, but improving your memory is very possible with the help of brain strengthening techniques, a healthier lifestyle, and the willpower to learn!

I challenge you to begin learning at least one of the methods you found to be the most intriguing to you in this book once you put it down. What do you have to lose? We could all greatly benefit from enhancing our brains power to recall information and events. As soon as next month

Photographic Memory

you can be living a life in better clarity than you have ever before in your life!

I hope that this book was fun to read and able to provide you with the tools you need to achieve brain-powered success!

Speed Reading

----- ❧☙ -----

How to Increase Your Reading Speed, Learning Abilities, and Comprehension

Logan G Davidson

Table of Contents

Introduction 107

Chapter 1:Ways to Eliminate Your Bad Reading Habits 109

Chapter 2:Skimming and Scanning Material .. 123

Chapter 3:Reading Words in Groups 135

Chapter 4:Painting the Words 145

Chapter 5: Pacer Techniques to Improve Speed Reading 155

Chapter 6:In-Depth Speed Reading 169

Chapter 7: Advancing Your Speed Reading Skills 183

Conclusion 195

Introduction

Congratulations on downloading *Speed Reading: How to Increase Your Reading Speed, Learning Abilities, and Comprehension,* and thank you for doing so.

The following chapters will discuss what speed reading is, how to break bad reading habits, techniques on how to successfully speed read, tips on reading effectively, and maintaining good reading comprehension.

The key difference between speed reading and normal reading is that in speed reading the reader uses visual thinking processes rather than auditory thinking processes as they read. Due to the fact that most people learn to read by saying the words aloud as they go, it is a common problem to become dependent on knowing how the words sound and on hearing what they sound like inside your head. Speed reading removes this almost completely, so you have to rely on how the words look.

Speed Reading

Speed reading, as we now know it, has been around for about sixty years. It has been used by many prominent figures including several United States presidents. There are a number of classes that have taught speed reading in schools, businesses, government, and universities.

The benefits of speed reading are widespread and will help you with more than just reading. By learning how to speed read you will eliminate bad reading habits, learn valuable study skills, improve visualization, increase reading comprehension, and of course, be able to read much quicker than you are currently able.

There are plenty of books on this subject on the market. Thanks again for choosing this one! Every effort was made to ensure it is full of as much useful information as possible. Please enjoy!

Chapter 1:
Ways to Eliminate Your Bad Reading Habits

Speed reading is a skill that, like any other skill, needs to be cultivated and learned over time. When we are young and first learning to read, however, we are not taught how to speed read. In fact, it's quite the opposite. As a child, you were likely taught how to read each word individually and to sound the words out verbally if they were not familiar. Although this is effective for young beginners, those habits are not effective for the long term.

Some of the main problems adults have with reading quickly stem from never having been taught how to read past these rudimentary steps. Habits such as subvocalization, rereading, inefficient reading, lack of concentration, and even poor breathing, or being uncomfortable while reading can lead to a lot of problems while trying to read quickly. These types of issues can also lead to frustration with reading and an unwillingness to read as an adult.

Speed Reading

Slow reading and an unwillingness to read can have serious consequences as an adult. Work, school, and personal life can all be affected. Productivity and comprehension go down while frustration goes up. For example, not being able to read a news article promptly could mean falling behind at work or school or failing to remain an informed citizen and facing embarrassment from peers.

However, it is only a matter of correcting habits and learning new techniques to improve your reading speed. Once new habits are well established, improvements in how you read and how much you get out of reading will be immediately noticeable.

On average, a person reads about two hundred to three hundred words per minute which at that speed, a person would take an entire eight-hour work day to finish reading a novel, a very slow pace indeed. What kind of difference would it make if you could double or triple that speed? Well, most people can make it to over one thousand words per minute with practice. What a feat! At that speed, it would only take two hours to read the same book. Some people can even make it well past that speed

Chapter 1: Ways to Eliminate Your Bad Reading Habits

mark to two or even three thousand words per minute. Although that is not a necessary goal for most people, imagine how much you could get done at that speed.

So, to begin your journey to becoming a faster and better reader, you should start by understanding why you have problems reading in the first place. Some of the easiest to correct problems involve being uncomfortable while reading. This could stem from needing prescription glasses or having an undiagnosed condition such as dyslexia or attention-deficit disorder (ADD.) If you are over thirty-five, chances are you will need reading glasses; there are fonts to aid dyslexia, and a wealth of advice on focusing with ADD is available. If something like this sounds like it might be the underlying cause of your inability to quickly read, be sure to address those issues before continuing to learn to speed read as you will not be able to make good progress and become disappointed.

Other ways of being uncomfortable while reading can stem from bad lighting, bad posture, forgetting to breathe, or moving the head while reading. Make sure before you start to read that you are in an adequately lit space, are sitting

Speed Reading

comfortably with the book at a proper height for back, shoulder, and neck support. You should not be hunching over your book. If you are using a computer to read or while reading, make sure everything is in a position where you do not have to keep moving your head up and down or side to side while working. This could easily cause neck strain and headaches.

Remember to breathe and eat right. This is a surprisingly common mistake, especially when studying intensely. Your brain needs oxygen and sugar to function correctly, and if you are hungry or not breathing well, you will not be able to focus or remember what you are reading later. You should develop the habit of breathing deeply from the diaphragm every few breaths to keep your brain in working condition and speed reading possible.

Another thing to keep in mind while reading is to keep a dictionary (digital or print) nearby. It is easier to remember what you are reading for the long term if you are not struggling with understanding the material. There is no reason not to look something up. Do not worry about being embarrassed for not knowing something. Don't become too focused on speed and focus on

Chapter 1: Ways to Eliminate Your Bad Reading Habits

improving. The exception to this rule is while first practicing to speed read. If you stop too much, you will never build the necessary muscle memory to read quickly. This is explained further in this chapter. However, reading without comprehension is pointless in the long run.

Make sure to eliminate all other distractions while reading especially when you are new to speed reading. Read in a quiet space, or use noise-cancelling headphones without music to stop background sounds from interrupting your focus. Music can be detrimental to focus so even if you think it helps, try reading without any playing while learning to speed read. It could be a bad habit that is actually making it harder for you to remain focused or remember what you are reading!

If you chronically have trouble focusing on what you are reading but don't' know why, don't worry because speed reading can help with that. When you are reading at a slow pace, your mind has more time to think of things besides what you are reading, and you can easily get lost in your own thoughts, and forget everything you read. Reading at a faster pace gives your mind less time to ponder other things. It's a lot harder to zone out while taking in more information.

After ensuring you are comfortable and removing distractions, look at which other bad habits you might have. A very common one that is a remnant of young reading skills is subvocalization. Subvocalization, otherwise known as silent speech, is internally reading a word out loud, imagining the sound. There are generally three types of subvocalization that are recognized.

1. Mouthing words as you read, almost reading vocally to yourself.

2. Imagining mouthing the words to yourself as you read without moving your mouth.

3. Being aware of how each word sounds but not waiting for them to be "spoken" internally before moving on.

Both of the first two are common with people who did not receive further instruction on how to read, which is usual in modern education and places a serious damper on how fast you can read. If you do either of the first two types of subvocalization, your reading speed is essentially

Chapter 1: Ways to Eliminate Your Bad Reading Habits

capped at one hundred fifty words per minute, well below the average, and your focus is too intent on the sounds of the words you are reading instead of their meaning. As you can see, subvocalizing too much is a bad habit that should be stopped sooner rather than later for more than just speed reading.

The third type is common however and much less of a detriment. There is no way to fully get rid of being aware of what the words you are reading sound like as you read them, and attempting to do so can hinder you. While reading, a reader can usually pick up on things like incomplete sentences and can point out that they missed reading part of the passage when they can "hear" how it is supposed to sound in their head. If you do not hear what the thing you are reading is supposed to sound like in your head, then you are moving past simple speed reading into skimming or scanning the material, which will be covered later in this book.

There are several ways for you to stop mouthing words while you read. These include putting a hand on the moving part of your face or throat which will make you aware that you are subvocalizing, making a sound or humming while you read to occupy the speech centers of the brain, and purposefully moving your eyes faster than you can vocalize the words. The most effective are usually the first two methods. The first of which allows you to become aware and consciously decide to stop subvocalizing. The second, making a sound while reading, also makes you aware of your subvocalization, but can be disorienting for those who learned to read word-by-word as it forces you to recognize words in a new way. All can be useful in stopping the bad habit so choose the one that works the best for you.

Another bad habit to work on is regression or rereading. Rereading is important in some ways, so it is not always a good thing to completely remove. However, it has a specific place in speed reading. Rereading is caused by not understanding something. Ultra-fast speed readers often lose track of what they are reading and must look randomly at a page, or even look backward in a book to catch meanings that they missed. However, an average speed reader should find an individual balance that works for them where they can understand the text with minimal rereading as it does slow you down. Unconscious rereading, or focusing on one spot

Chapter 1: Ways to Eliminate Your Bad Reading Habits

too long, is also a common problem but easily fixed.

A good rule of thumb to avoid rereading is to understand that most authors usually explain something further in the text, so it is not always necessary to backtrack. If you still do not understand after a few paragraphs, you might have missed something, and it may be necessary to go back. Another tool you can use is reading while moving your finger or another object along the text to keep you focused on moving forward. This is called pacing and will be covered in more detail later in this book.

One of the most common mistakes with beginning speed readers is that they start too fast. If you are reading past your ability, you will need to reread more often so be sure to work your way up with practice until you can almost eliminate the need to reread.

To practice breaking bad habits and getting into speed reading, you should use a large print book that is not essential reading material. Using a large print book will help you move quicker and remain focused longer. Also, as a new speed reader, you will inevitably miss information as you read since you are trying new things. This is not a problem, but for that reason, you should pick something that you do not need to understand completely as focusing too much on comprehension will slow you down and hinder your speed reading.

Focusing on comprehension will come later. In fact, you should be reading faster than you are currently comfortable. This is not to be confused with simply running through the book and not remembering anything. As instructed above, you cannot start too fast, and comprehension is important. Keep some sticky notes or a highlighter nearby or dog-ear pages you want to come back to if you need to, but don't stop moving forward in the book.

You should also be practicing your new techniques every day. Try setting aside at least fifteen minutes a day where you can be free from distractions and be comfortable to read. Just like an athlete learning a new skill, your new reading techniques will take time to adjust to and to form a solid muscle memory. Don't be discouraged if it takes time to learn, or you don't catch everything! Eventually, your brain will catch up to the new speed.

Chapter 1: Ways to Eliminate Your Bad Reading Habits

If you pay attention to the paths your eyes take while reading, you might notice that it is inefficient. Your eyes make snapshots as you read, and making too many by focusing on each word will slow you down. Try looking at multiple words in a row as you read, grouping them. This is called chunking and will be covered later in this book.

After addressing your bad habits, if you have any, there are some things to keep in mind as you move forward in your speed reading journey that will build new, better reading habits. Begin by taking a good look at what you are reading before you start. Why are you reading this particular book or article? What are you going to get out of it? You need to take note of genre and purpose. If you are only reading for fun, you do not have to speed through it unless you want to. (There is no shame in speed reading novels when there are so many out there!) If you are reading something where you need to know specific bits of information like names or dates, it might also not be the time to speed read. Regardless, take note of why you are reading something as it will affect how you read to get what you need out of the text.

Speed Reading

After understanding the purpose that you are reading for, take time to pre-read the book. This will only take about ten minutes, but will greatly increase your understanding and ability to get through the material quickly especially in the case of textbooks. Go over the information on the cover and dust jacket including the summary, reviews, and author information. Then, take a look at the contents, bibliography, or index to get a picture of what will be covered. Finally, flip through a few pages of the book, glancing at pictures, diagrams, section titles, or chapter summaries, if available.

Look at the book as an opportunity. To truly read effectively, you cannot look at the book like it has everything upfront for you. Books, articles, and poems all have messages that go beyond the surface of the text. Take note that it is your responsibility as a reader to refine the material presented and make something of it. Do not be a passive reader.

Work your way up in speed using the above methods, improving on new habits, and breaking bad ones. No one expects you to be perfect at a new skill right away so do not be critical if you only get one step at a time.

Chapter 1: Ways to Eliminate Your Bad Reading Habits

After breaking all of your bad habits, learning new techniques, and practice, you will become much more efficient and faster as a reader. It may be uncomfortable to change at first, but if you stick to it, you will surely be surprised by the results. By making speed reading a habit, you can then once again focus on comprehension and make it a lifelong skill.

The rest of this book will show you some other ways to read quickly and how to improve your reading skills as a whole by covering how to skim and scan through material for quicker coverage, reading words in groups to increase speed, increasing comprehension through visualization, and how to continue your journey towards being a full-fledged speed reader.

Chapter 2: Skimming and Scanning Material

Speed reading can be extremely helpful, but sometimes there are needs for even quicker coverage of material and an understanding of when to skip less necessary passages. Skimming and scanning are useful in these situations. Skimming is a technique of viewing a section of text to form a summary of the material, and scanning is a technique of searching a section of text for useful information and extracting main ideas using a mind map. They are very similar, but the goals and outcomes of each are different. Utilizing both makes you a much more flexible reader.

Let us start by covering skimming in more detail. Skimming usually involves reading the beginning and end of the book or chapter, the first sentence of each paragraph, and other points like graphs and tables in an attempt to understand the main points of the information, and know where to find the necessary details to answer your questions. It gives you an overview of the text.

Some people can do this easily, but others need the practice to gain this skill. It is usually not something that is done until adulthood. It is not an advisable technique for information-rich text unless the intent is to use skimming as a pre-reading technique because full comprehension can be adversely affected.

The best times to skim are to pre-read, review information after reading, to take main points from sections you don't want to read, or to find relevant sources while researching. During these times, skimming can save you a lot of time.

Skimming can produce good results when the time is tight, but care should be taken to go slow enough to still understand the material presented. Using skimming techniques can aid in comprehension especially when it is coupled with other speed-reading techniques, and it is most often used when researching to gain an understanding of a text without having to waste time reading every article or book in its entirety to determine its usefulness.

Chapter 2: Skimming and Scanning Material

Main points of a text can be understood quickly using skimming, sometimes even better than after normal reading. This is likely because all the main ideas are read in rapid succession without being bogged down by less important sections. Comprehension increases further than normal reading when a reader skims a text and notes areas of importance before reading. This technique is extremely useful for students or those reading technical works as studying and understanding the information is easier with a primer on the topic and an idea of what to pay close attention to.

Use caution when skimming, however, because unlike simple speed reading alone, when you skip material, you can potentially miss something important or deeper meanings in what you are reading. Skimming is a good speed reading skill to overview or review textbooks or for research in particular.

To skim effectively, pay attention to the parts of the book listed above, but do not give equal weight to all of them. In addition to the introduction and conclusion of sections and the first sentence of paragraphs, look for bold or italic type, bulleted or numbered lists, keywords and phrases related to the topic at hand, charts and tables, names or dates that may be important, and unfamiliar words. If you find something you think is important, take a few extra seconds to read the entire paragraph it is in. If time is too tight, such as before a test, prioritize chapter overviews or summaries and bold text words.

The skill in skimming comes from knowing what to read or not to read and which method to use to most effectively pull information from the text in little time. It works the best with non-fiction material, but if your research involves fiction literature, it can still be a useful tactic. Like more basic speed reading, this is also a skill that takes time to perfect.

Examples of Uses of Skimming

The main use for skimming, as explained above, is research. Imagine doing research on a topic that interests you. If you start by reading a few paragraphs, you can get an idea of what the whole topic is about, and what keywords or phrases are important to look for. After that, you can start to look at the start of each paragraph, charts, tables, etc., and only look deeper if

Chapter 2: Skimming and Scanning Material

something seems important. After each beginning sentence, be sure to glance over the rest of the text for the keywords you have already discovered. Read conclusions and introductions more thoroughly. Make sure to inventory what you are learning to ensure you are grasping the material. If you aren't getting the main ideas, then you are not skimming well.

Another use is if you have already found a wealth of information on a topic, but do not have time to read every word like in the case of a presentation or paper that is due in a few days. By skimming, you can read everything in much less time.

The same goes for reviewing for a test. Skimming can allow you to home in on information that you do not already know and only study those sections. It is a time saver!

To decide if it is an appropriate time to skim read, understand the following points:

- The material should most likely be non-fiction

- Skimming is useful to save time. If you have time to read, skimming might not be necessary

- It should only be used when skipping some material is not detrimental

- You should not be reading things that you already understand while skimming

Now let's take a look at what scanning is. Scanning, while reading, is a technique of searching a section of text for useful information and of extracting main ideas using a mind map. A mind map is a way of organizing what you are reading hierarchically based on relevance, and it increases the readers' ability to retrieve information from the text. Scanning is usually done in conjunction with skimming to get more out of the text while studying.

Scanning alone is a speed reading tactic that lets you locate and pick out individual bits of information from what you are reading very quickly. You can think of skimming as snorkeling in the reefs and scanning as deep-sea diving for treasure. You get much deeper information with scanning, but your area of focus must be smaller.

Chapter 2: Skimming and Scanning Material

With skimming, like snorkeling, your goal is to cover a lot of material and find what is important. With scanning, you know what is important and are looking for something in particular.

Scanning is what you do if after skimming, you find that the information is relevant. You are looking for keywords and cues within the text at this point. While scanning a book or article, make sure to only look for one keyword at a time. Looking for more will make you unable to keep track, and you will miss what you are looking for. It is a quick process, so it is smart just to do multiple scans. Like with skimming, if something seems important, read the surrounding text more closely.

Learning to scan is pretty easy since most people do it without even noticing it in their daily lives. Make sure to establish what you want to accomplish while scanning before doing so then locate the appropriate material and understand how it is structured. Knowing how the information is structured in what you are reading can give you an advantage on knowing where to look. An example will be if a list is in an alphabetical or a numerical order.

Speed Reading

Some tips for scanning are to use your finger to focus where you want to look on a page and to use your peripheral vision to check more words at a time for what you are looking for. Both of these techniques can allow you to scan quicker. For example, while looking for a word in a dictionary, use your finger to trail down the words until you find what you need, and use your peripheral vision to be able to move quickly down the list.

Remember that keywords are the primary factor while scanning to speed read! You need to keep what you are looking for in mind the entire time.

Examples of Uses of Scanning

One of the best times to use scanning while speed reading or instead of speed reading is to answer a specific question. In this case, you already know what keywords or phrases you are looking for so skimming is not essential, and you can just start scanning for what you need. Read all questions you have for the text before starting and choose which keywords you will look for one at a time. Make sure to scan for each one individually! Once you have found what you are

Chapter 2: Skimming and Scanning Material

looking for, read the rest closer. Then reread your question to make sure the information is pertinent.

There are other times where you scan and probably didn't even realize you were doing so! The television guide, a newspaper, social media, using a dictionary, the shelf at a store, a list of results in a search engine, the index of a book, or even your notes are common things that we scan daily as readers. These things all have predictable structures and can be covered quickly if you are looking for something specific, or if you want to get to the point without having to stop and read everything.

A downfall of scanning is that it can be tiring due to how much concentration is required. If you let other thoughts take over while scanning, you have to start all over so make sure to use the advice in this book on how to concentrate and stay comfortable while reading as you scan.

"Natural" Speed Readers

People who speed read without being taught often use a modified way of skimming and scanning which they claim to see an entire paragraph or a page at once and can pull keywords and points out much quicker than usual. Your eye can reasonably see an area a few words high and a few words wide. These people use that to their advantage while looking at the text to pull keywords and important points quicker than the usual pace. Every time their eyes land on the page, they are getting an entire chunk of what is written.

Essentially, they are lessening the number of fixation points they need while reading. Some people focus on each word at a time; others focus on a few at a time while these "natural" speed readers are focusing on an entire clump of words at once. Using this technique, they can put a mental picture together of what is being said on a page, sometimes up to five lines at a time! To put this into perspective, these speed readers can scan up to ten or more times faster than a taught speed reader who is using pacing techniques.

These readers hardly even use benchmarks like words per minute since their system can vary widely between sections of a book. Since some parts are more relevant than others, they can pick and choose what to focus on. This is different than simple speed reading but has many similarities to skimming and scanning. In

Chapter 2: Skimming and Scanning Material

speed reading alone, you travel across the page at an almost even pace regardless of what is written, whereas, in skimming and scanning, you choose the most relevant information and focus on it.

Although the average reader couldn't hope to read at these superhuman reading speeds, a lesson can be learned from them. Simple speed reading alone is not as efficient as knowing when to skip over something or when to linger on more important sections. That is where skimming and scanning become important to the speed reading process. Be sure to keep these techniques for speed reading in mind as you move forward.

Chapter 3:
Reading Words in Groups

Probably the most important, but also the most difficult speed reading technique to master if you really want to read quickly, is clustering (otherwise known as chunking.) Clustering is when you read words in groups. While you learn to read, you are taught to read one word at a time, taking in each one individually. While this works for a while, if you really want to read quickly, the way to do so is to break this habit. You should be able to read up to four or more words at once in just a glance with practice.

While you read, your eyes naturally create fixation points. These points are where your eyes stop for a minuscule moment before they keep moving. If you create a fixation point on every word, it will slow down your reading speed. As you practice reading, you should start to lessen the number of fixation points you create naturally with an increase in vocabulary and the ability to recognize common words quicker. Not everyone gains this skill as they grow up though. However, there is a way to practice this skill and improve it or to begin learning how to utilize it as an adult.

You might not even realize that you cluster words. While going down the street, you might read a common city name like "New York City" all in one go, even if you read each word individually just now in print. It is not always something that we dobut is achievable with practice just like the other speed reading techniques in this book. That being said, do not be discouraged if it takes time, or one technique just isn't working for you. All these methods of speed reading can be useful, but not all of them are for everyone.

To practice clustering words, pick something light to read such as a large-print fiction novel that was recommended in chapter one. Try speed reading it with the tools you already have. You might notice you do some clustering already but to continue, concentrate on trying to link two to four words. After that, try to reread it and see what you missed. Continue practicing this by reading a section at a time and repeating the process.

Chapter 3: Reading Words in Groups

Once you notice that you can speed read while not missing much, it means that your natural reading speed has increased. This might take a while, but keep at it! Any skill worth learning is a skill worth putting time into. Keep in mind that this speed reading technique might take the longest to master.

Once you get comfortable with that speed, you can try to improve further with the two-fixation technique. This is exactly what it sounds like. You only make two fixation points per line of text. This is an advanced technique, but if you are truly dedicated to speed reading, it will be worth your time. Use your finger or a pen as a guide to help. If you are having trouble, work up to two fixations by starting with three per line. If you have practiced this skill using the steps above, you likely already have about three or four fixations a line!

Another more advanced way to practice clustering is to take a page of text and make two lines approximately two words from the beginning of each line and two words from the end of each line down the page. Then use those as guidelines to stay between while reading. This will train your peripheral vision by making you

Speed Reading

skip focusing on those words and make you only see them in groups. It will train your eyes to stay in the middle of the page. This method is called triple-chunking.

If you are having trouble with the two-fixation technique described above in this chapter, start triple-chunking, then advance to double-chunking by drawing the line down the middle of the page. Dividing the page in half after getting used to the triple-chunk guidelines will make you take each half in one chunk. These methods will help you if you have trouble with correcting your fixation.

To advance your skill in reading groups of words further, try the zig-zag method. This method pairs pacing which will be covered later in this book with clustering by moving your finger or other object down the page in a zig-zag movement. The goal of this exercise is to ignore less important words and only focus on words like nouns and verbs. This technique is very similar to skimming or scanning and can even be used in conjunction with those other skills. Do not try this unless you are comfortable with the above methods.

Chapter 3: Reading Words in Groups

If you want to use a computer to practice, try AccelaReader.com. This website can help you with both simple speed reading and chunking. You start by inputting the text that you want to read by pasting it in. Try something like a news article or a short story. You can set your reading speed and how many words you wish to be shown at once as well as helpful settings like font size and color. Then you just click "read," and it will flash words for you to read. Try it without chunking, then up the number of words shown to two or three at a time to try chunking. If you feel confident, try four!

Besides this one website, there are also several desktops or mobile applications available. Try several to see which you like. With a mobile app, you can even practice speed reading in your spare time like while riding the bus or waiting in line. You can also find printable practice sheets that have the words already chunked if the in-print practice is more your style.

To practice chunking, regardless of if you prefer print or digital practice, make sure to set aside several minutes a day where you can practice without distraction. Make sure to work your way up to speed. If you skip forward too much, you are likely to get frustrated and want to quit.

Also, do not try to practice for too long in one sitting. Your eye muscles will get tired, and your progression and learning of the skill will dampen. You wouldn't start training for a marathon by running a marathon; you would start by running at a pace that you could achieve. The same goes for speed reading.

A good tip is to move your fixation point from the word to the point between the words. Using just this method alone will likely double your reading speed.

Just like the other speed reading techniques discussed in this book, you can combine chunking with pacing, skimming, or scanning to reach even quicker reading speeds. Once you master all of them, you will be a faster, more flexible reader who can pick which methods to use based on need. Although chunking is the most difficult of them all, it is useful for quickly reading things like novels or news articles where you want to read the entire piece but want to do so as quickly as possible to save time. Reading

Chapter 3: Reading Words in Groups

multiple words at once could allow you to reach speeds of up to one thousand words per minute with practice.

A great aspect of chunking is that it does not as greatly affect reading comprehension like skimming and scanning because you are reading the whole thing. While you practice, you will inevitably miss some information, but as your skill increases so do your comprehension.

Another big plus to chunking is the reduction in subvocalization. If you have trouble with that bad habit, this might be the skill for you to focus on. It automatically makes you unable to read to yourself because you are reading too fast to focus on individual words.

Just like a single letter does not convey the meaning of the whole word, a single word does not convey the whole meaning of a sentence. Using chunking can help increase your ability to understand the material when used correctly. Being able to recognize more than one word at once allows you to grasp more of the author's meaning at once.

A comprehensive list of reasons to learn to cluster read by reading words in groups is below.

Speed Reading

Benefits of Reading Words in Groups

- Increases vocabulary and comprehension through learning to recognize words quicker

- Visualization of what you are reading becomes easier

- Works well with other speed reading methods

- Helps to remove bad habits especially sub-vocalization

- Reduces inefficient eye movements

- Allows you to understand the gist of what you are reading quickly

- Promotes the ignoring of filler words and puts the focus on verbs and nouns

- Improves comprehension

As you can see, there are a wide array of good reasons to try clustering while speed reading. It discourages bad habits and helps to build new ones as well as builds upon simple speed reading

Chapter 3: Reading Words in Groups

and other reading techniques to make you a more fluid and capable reader.

Please note, that in the first chapter, it was mentioned that if you need prescription eyeglasses, you should take care of that prior to attempting to speed read. Clustering is a major part of the reasoning for that advice. You will need to be able to use all parts of your vision to speed read especially while attempting to read groups of words at the same time. You need good focus and peripheral vision, and having glasses will also save you from eye strain and headaches that will distract you while reading.

Chapter 4:
Painting the Words

Reading is not a passive activity. Unfortunately, not everyone is taught how to be an active reader, and they suffer for it. Being a passive reader results in reading being boring and the material difficult to understand and remember. Many people suffer from this as they age and begin to hate reading.

Some people see reading as boring because they do not see it as an active activity like playing games or watching a movie, but as a passive activity where they have to allow the book to speak for itself. This is not the case as all texts have several layers of meaning and can be interpreted in multiple ways. Many people have very different ideas of what characters in a story actually looks like!

In fact, one of the best ways to become an active reader is visualizing what you are reading. To some this may come naturally; to others, it needs to be a learned skill. The following paragraphs will explain what visualizing is, how to visualize while reading, and the benefits of being able to visualize from reading comprehension and your ability to speed read.

Visualization is the ability to form an image in your mind about what you are reading. This is sometimes thought of as making a personal movie inside of your head and sometimes thought of as making "word pictures" of what is going on. This skill enables a reader to better engage with what is written.

Visualization can be described as turning what you are reading into a more tangible version. For example, if you are reading a scene in a fiction novel while visualizing what is going on, you might "see" the scene and characters and "hear" the dialogue as you move through the text. For this reason, people good at visualizing often compare it to making a movie or a picture in their minds. This skill takes a simple series of words and transforms it into something much more interesting.

Visualizing while reading is best taught while first learning to read. Unfortunately, this does not always happen. If you have trouble

Chapter 4: Painting the Words

visualizing, hopefully, this guide will help you improve and learn to enjoy reading in a new and exciting way.

There are some factors that can halt or put a damper on learning how to visualize while reading. The main reasons are a lack of background knowledge and a lack of personal interest in what is being read. Prior knowledge is underrated but important while reading both fiction and non-fiction because a reader cannot picture what is going on or is being discussed without a frame of reference. This is more difficult with non-fiction since gaining background knowledge on a topic prior to seeing it in something like a textbook is difficult.

Feeling involved with what you are reading is also very important especially for young readers. It is common for teachers to see students view reading as a chore instead of something useful or fun. Visualization could help these young readers enjoy and get more out of reading.

If you have trouble visualizing, it may be a good idea to slow down and work on this skill separately from speed reading before incorporating it into your new speed reading toolkit. Learning to visualize and speed read at the same time may be overwhelming.

This book has already referenced some ways to become a more active reader such as understanding the genre and purpose of what you are reading and asking questions about what you are reading. Visualizing is also key to becoming a more active reader, and something that is key to speed reading.

How to Visualize:

There are many visualization exercises that you can do to practice this skill, if necessary. Many experts recommend a set of four exercises called the picture exercise, the object exercise, the person exercise, and the place exercise. These four visualization techniques can help you learn or improve your visualization abilities while reading and greatly improve your reading comprehension. Before trying any of the activities described below, make sure you have adequate time and a place without distractions so you can maintain focus.

Start with the easiest one, the picture exercise; find a picture of an object and study it very closely. After you feel like you have a good

Chapter 4: Painting the Words

image of the picture in your head, close your eyes and attempt to recreate it. Try to remember every detail you can from the colors to textures to shapes. Open your eyes after that, and see how your image matches to the original. Repeat this exercise as many times as you find necessary.

Next, move on to the object exercise. Locate an object near you, and study it closely. Take in as many details about the object as possible. Now close your eyes, and try to visualize the object. Recreate the feeling, appearance, smell, etc., using as many senses as possible. A good object to try this method with is food as it will allow you to recreate in your imagination all five senses worth of information. Be as specific as possible. What is the texture? Does it smell good? What is the temperature?

There are infinite possibilities but focus on details. Do not let irrelevant things interrupt the process.

After using an object that is near you and recreating it in your mind, try doing the same thing with something that is familiar to you but not present. For example, close your eyes, relax, and attempt to visualize the experience of eating your favorite food. Include as much detail as possible. Repeat this with new things until you have the hang of it.

Next, move on to the person exercise. Choose someone you know very well like a good friend or a family member. Make sure you know the person well enough to recognize them even when they are far away. Relax, close your eyes, and visualize them in your mind. Focus on the details of their face and bodies from several directions. This will be much harder than the previous exercises. After you have a clear picture in your mind of the person, try changing their situation, clothes, expression, or hairstyle. Repeat this with several people.

The last exercise is the place exercise. Think of a location or an environment and visualize yourself there. Again, focus on all the details you can. Utilize every sense you have to create a complete image of the location including sounds and smells. Repeat this with a new location, or change the season of the one you already visualized.

Another way to practice visualization is to take one of the above scenes or items that you

Chapter 4: Painting the Words

visualized and imagine attempting to explain what you see and feel to someone over the phone. Use as much descriptive language as possible. Can you adequately describe something as well as you see it? Probably not. This is why visualization is important while reading. You can never get the entire picture without it.

Here are some other ways to improve your visualization. Read sentence by sentence, and picture what is happening in each one individually as you go. While reading, imagine what is happening is more like a documentary or a film that you are watching. What would it be like if it was animated? Try to record reading something aloud to yourself, then replay it to see if your visualization changes after hearing it.

Sometimes, drawing can help as well. Try to draw out what a character is doing, or how two or more characters are interacting. Don't worry about how it looks since it is only for your reference. Drawing can also be very effective for non-fiction text. Try to illustrate what is going on in a technical work with diagrams or charts or connect ideas and themes with lines.

Speed Reading

Remember to utilize past experiences while reading to create a fuller picture of what is happening. Make the text personal and interesting with sensory images like in the practice examples above. It will ultimately aid your recollection of what you are reading.

Benefits of Visualization While Reading:

- Necessary for good reading comprehension

- Aids concentration

- Improves willingness to read

- Helpful for overcoming bad reading habits like subvocalization by redirecting attention to the entire text while distracting from the sounds of individual words

- Helpful for learning to cluster read

- Essential in learning to become an active reader

- Strengthen your ability to learn new material through reading

Chapter 4: Painting the Words

- Improve long-term memory of what is read

Importance of Visualization in Speed Reading:

Visualization is most often associated with reading fiction, and speed reading is most often associated with reading non-fiction so you may be wondering what use visualization has in speed reading. Well, as listed above, it is important for comprehension, concentration, overcoming bad reading habits, learning to cluster read, being an active reader, and to improve your long-term memory while reading. The most important being the aid of stopping subvocalization. Although all of these are important to take into consideration if you think that making images of what is going on might be unrelated to your goals, that's not all there is to it.

Reading fiction is usually best read in natural time to best experience everything the book has to offer which is usually contrary to speed reading. However, speed reading can help while reading fiction too. Most novels have long descriptive scenes that can be read more quickly using speed reading techniques while the more important parts like dialogue can be read in real time.

Also, without the ability to visualize, you do not have the ability to understand what is being read as quickly as those who utilize good visualization. As a reader, you can zip through emotional scenes much easier with visualization.

Chapter 5:
Pacer Techniques to Improve Speed Reading

Up until now, this book has mentioned pacing several times. This chapter will be dedicated to explaining in detail what pacing is, how it developed, and how the technique will help to improve your reading speed. The techniques explained earlier in this book are varied and aid in reducing bad habits, building new reading habits, improving comprehension, and of course, building speed. However, none of those is as important to gaining the desired speed in speed reading than pacing. Remember that pacing is the only technique in this book that is used to speed read that was developed for speed reading only.

Pacing methods vary from person-to-person and are also called meta guiding. Pacing while reading is a way of guiding where your eyes fall on the page by using a finger or another pointer, such as a pen, to move faster through the text. This, of course, works only with printed text, but if you wish to practice pacing on something that is not in print, there are techniques related to pacing that will also be explained later in this chapter. You may also print what you wish to read yourself if you have access to a printer.

To pace or guide yourself while reading, your finger or other pacing tools should be moving fairly rapidly across the lines of text. This will surely be faster than you are comfortable with at first at around five hundred words per minute with around four fixations per line. To put that into perspective, an average reader can read about two hundred fifty words per minute with about eight fixation points per line. At this speed, you will likely not have a high level of comprehension, but that is okay. Your comprehension will improve with practice and with combining this tool with the other techniques you have learned in this book.

Pushing yourself to where you are uncomfortable at first is an exercise the same as an athlete exercising to improve. Think of it as adding some weight to your lift regimen or some distance while training for a marathon. You probably will not succeed at first, but with practice, your new skill will become easier until

Chapter 5: Pacer Techniques to Improve Speed Reading

you no longer notice the extra weight or distance that you added. In that way, work your way up to moving at five hundred words per minute which is a good pace to ensure both speed and retention. After a while and more practice, you may become comfortable moving even faster.

Reading faster than you are currently able to will affect many equate to changing speeds in a car. If you start off going at a rate of thirty miles per hour on a city street, get on the freeway and increase to sixty miles per hour, then exit the freeway and slow back down, the lower speed of thirty miles per hour seems slow, whereas it was normal before. This feeling makes readers slowly increase their speed naturally. Using the same analogy, the next time you start reading, thirty-five miles per hour will feel normal.

As you practice pacing, remember that speed reading is a skill that has to be practiced daily to see improvement. Think of it as working on your speed reading stamina. This has been mentioned several times in this book so far because it is important. Chances are, if you stop practicing, you will become discouraged and stop. Most people who set out on a journey to learn this skill will stop before they reach their goals because it takes longer than they expect. Do not hope for instant results!

To start learning how to use a pacer, you should pick a pacer that you are comfortable with. A pacer can be anything that you can use to sweep along the page under words to keep your attention on moving forward. If you do not want to use your finger, a pen or pencil, a chopstick, or a paper can be used. A finger, pen, or pencil are the most common choices. Also, when using a writing utensil, you can easily and quickly mark interesting or important parts to come back to later. Regardless of which item you use as a pacer, just move it smoothly across the page as you go. Even if you do not increase your speed by much, it will still increase focus.

The steps outlined above obviously will not do you much good when reading on a computer screen. Moving your hand across the screen of a tablet, phone, or a computer is strange, not useful, and often impossible. If you use an external mouse, you can use that as a workaround for a traditional pacer by moving it on the screen as you go. Do not try this with a laptop trackpad as its movements will be jerky and uneven and not help with focus at all.

Chapter 5: Pacer Techniques to Improve Speed Reading

Besides using a mouse if you want to read digitally, you might want to try using a speed reading application or a website and input the text you want to read. An example was explained earlier in this book, AccelaReader.com. If you read a lot digitally, this is a highly recommended technique to read faster.

Why an application or website such as AccelaReader.com works is a technology called Rapid Serial Visual Presentation or RSVP reading. This type of reading is an experimental model that keeps you moving forward by flashing or streaming your words rather than drawing attention to them the way print-based pacing works. Both are effective in improving your speed, and it is important to choose which one works best for you.

While RSVP reading, inefficient eye movements, moving across the page, and page-turning have been removed from the experience which could help you read even faster than in print. It allows you as a reader to see an unlimited number of words in a limited position. RSVP reading also removers distractors that can be on the rest of a page of text. RSVP reading might be a good choice for speed reading if you have trouble holding books, or the movement of traditional pacing is impossible for you such as in the case of disability or arthritis.

Keep in mind that there are two types of RSVP reading; static and moving. In static RSVP reading, the words are shown sequentially and in the same location and then disappear for the next word. A disadvantage of this type of RSVP reading is that there is no time to validate what you have seen before the word is removed. This is a good way to stop rereading and fixation but can hinder your comprehension.

In moving RSVP reading, the words appear serially, move across a display, and then disappear. In both modes, the words have the same entry and exit points and are shown at the same rates. In moving RSVP, it is common to see the words stream across the screen horizontally, but diagonal and ring systems also exist. This type is also more akin to traditional pacing methods.

Below is a step-by-step outline on how to speed read with a pacer.

How to use a Pacer to Speed Read:

Chapter 5: Pacer Techniques to Improve Speed Reading

- Pick your pacer; your finger, pen, or a slip of paper will all work.

- Start reading at your normal speed using the pacer.

- Increase your reading speed until you are no longer able to understand the material and feel the need to reread easily.

- Slow back down until just before that point, and try reading for several minutes at that new speed.

- Reread the section at your old speed to test comprehension and feel how much faster you were able to read.

- Repeat this process, starting a little faster each day.

You may be wondering how the pacing method was developed. After all, isn't using your finger to move along text something children do while learning to read? Wouldn't it be counterintuitive to go back to that method? Pacing techniques were developed by Evelyn Wood in the late 1950's and were the first method to learn how to speed read developed specifically for speed reading. Wood was a teacher and researcher who wanted to understand how speed reading worked and why some people could read quicker than others. She even tried to force herself to read quicker.

After nothing she tried seemed to work, she almost gave up. However, she happened to notice that moving her hand across a book drew the attention of her eyes and decided to try using it as a technique to keep her focused on moving forward in an attempt to gain speed. Thus the pacer was discovered.

How Pacing Improves Speed Reading:

Pacing methods can reduce bad habits while reading such as sub-vocalization and regression, work well with other speed reading techniques, and also improve focus. As we have covered extensively in this book, bad reading habits can and will slow you down and should be corrected to speed read successfully. Pacing is a great help with that process, most notably with subvocalization and inefficient reading due to fixations and regression.

Chapter 5: Pacer Techniques to Improve Speed Reading

To review, subvocalization is internally reading a word out loud, imagining the sound. This is common because of how we are taught to read as children but can be corrected with practice. Pacing can help a lot with stopping subvocalization by having you read faster than you can vocally read to yourself. Many people who had a problem with subvocalization have helped themselves read faster and get more out of reading by using a pacer alone.

Regression, otherwise called rereading, is caused by not understanding something and fixating on certain words for too long and is caused by a lack of focus. Both are common, and pacing can help. When you feel the need to look back while reading, you stop, break focus, and need time to regroup. Think about it as someone taking a walk. The person who keeps going from point a to point b will arrive much quicker than the person stopping at points c, d, and e along the way.

All of these stops while reading is unnecessary and becomes less common as your reading skill increases naturally due to things like increasing vocabulary and better visualization. They add up to a lot of wasted time while reading so building better habits soon is a good idea. However, to break the habit, pacing can help. Besides the obvious key to reducing fixations by forcing yourself not to stop reading, using a pacer can also help you not need to reread material. Reading quicker helps most people focused and keeps what you read pages ago fresh in mind.

Speaking of focusing while reading, that is likely the best part of using a pacer to read. With all the distractions that can happen when you are trying to read, staying focused is key. This is especially important when you are not practicing in a distraction-free location and are trying to read at work, school, or another public location. Your phone, social media, music, and other people talking can easily derail your train of thought. If you can't avoid these distractions, a pacer can help to draw your focus back to what you are reading.

Pacing also works well with other speed reading techniques. The techniques to improve your reading you have learned about in this book so far are skimming, scanning, clustering, and visualization. As you know, skimming is a technique of viewing a section of text to form a

Chapter 5: Pacer Techniques to Improve Speed Reading

summary of the material, and scanning is a technique of searching a section of text for useful information and extracting main ideas using a mind map. Both of these speed reading techniques benefit greatly when you focus where you want to look with a pacer. They also immensely aid in the speed reading process when done prior to reading and allow you to speed read more efficiently.

Clustering is when you read words in groups. Clustering and using a pacer to speed read might as well be two sides of the same coin and are amazing tools to use at the same time. If you can master clustering words and minimize your fixation points to just two or three per line, then using a pacer to keep you focused, your reading speed will increase by a wide margin indeed.

When you use these two techniques in conjunction with each other, you may notice that you change how you use your pacer. At first, while pacing, your pacer will run from one side of the page to the other. However, when combined with grouping words, you will probably start the line a few words in and end the line a few words back before jumping to the next line. You might also learn to skip focusing on filler words.

Visualization is the ability to form an image in your mind about what you are reading. Visualization is a very important ability to have cultivated for speed reading since it allows you to understand what is being read much quicker than those who cannot utilize good visualization. When using a pacer, you might lose the meaning of what is written if you cannot form an image of it and connect to it on a deeper, more emotional level while reading.

Another benefit of using a pacer to speed read is that it adds a physical movement into the experience. It has been proven that movement can aid in learning and recollection. Linking the movement of your pacer with reading makes the material you are reading easier to remember by embedding it deeper into your memory. This doesn't only work with physical movement. Any other senses you can use while reading will also help you remember what you are reading easier.

Overall, learning to use a pacer to speed read effectively is very important. It will allow you to break some bad habits as well as build upon

Chapter 5: Pacer Techniques to Improve Speed Reading

better reading skills. Pacing will also aid your recollection when done correctly.

Although using a pacer might feel like a childish skill, do not shy away from it on your journey towards being a speed reader. As explained above, there are many great reasons to use a pacer. In fact, pacing yourself while reading should be your main tool since it is the only technique developed solely for the purpose of speed while reading.

Chapter 6:
In-Depth Speed Reading

By now you have read about eliminating bad reading habits, skimming and scanning for quick overviews and studying, reading words in groups (clustering) to reduce fixation points, improving visualization to aid reading comprehension, and how to use a pacer to increase reading speed. That is quite a bit of information, and you will surely increase your reading speed with practice using those techniques. However, there is still more you can learn about speed reading! This chapter will cover the history of speed reading and a host of tips on how to improve your reading comprehension and speed.

The History of Speed Reading:

Speed reading became well known in 1957 when Evelyn Wood's Reading Dynamics program was introduced. You read about Evelyn Wood in the previous chapter. She invented

Speed Reading

speed reading as we now know it with the discovery of using a pacer to read.

John F. Kennedy even had Wood's teachers teach the process of speed reading in the White House. Presidents Nixon and Carter also learned how to speed read. Jimmy Carter applauded the system as a big help in getting through several hundred pages of information a day and aiding him in making decisions as a president.

Almost every speed reading system ever created and taught begins with speed- building exercises which are built to remove bad reading habits and pacing as a key component to speed reading. It is known, however, that only doing speed exercises is not enough, and the most successful programs also show you other methods of improving your reading skill. This book strives to do all of that to make you a well-rounded and flexible reader.

However, for a lot of the history of speed reading, this wasn't the case. Classes were taught only using the speed exercises method. They lauded the importance of words per minute without the new thinking techniques to maintain reading comprehension. When students were

Chapter 6: In-Depth Speed Reading

done with the classes they had learned very little. Slowly, programs with a more sophisticated understanding of reading have emerged due to the need for understanding to match speed while reading. Now, any program that focuses solely on words per minute is regarded with caution.

Most academic studies done since speed reading rose to prominence have concluded that reading comprehension goes down when readers speed read. These usually only have the speed reader reading at several times the pace of a normal reader without allowing for the other techniques speed readers use to increase their understanding and often use standards which are not realistic for an average reader in the real world. For these reasons, these studies should be regarded with caution. Each individual should see if speed reading works for them and their purpose while reading.

Historically, most college classes teach that reading something once is not usually enough to learn it. That is why study skills teachers will say that speed reading is a terrible thing and that speed reading does nothing for reading comprehension. This is true in some ways. Since a lot of speed reading courses have historically failed to teach how to read well besides speed reading, study skills classes are right to question its place in learning. Speed reading alone blasts your short-term memory but fails to commit what is read to long-term memory.

Following the advice in this book, and using speed reading to study should be no problem. By the time you have finished reading, you will have learned how to skim and scan, remain focused, and have learned several studying techniques that you can deploy while speed reading.

Improving Your Reading Skills Further:

As you already know, speed reading is a skill that has to be practiced. This means that you can keep on improving for a long time. One way that you can continue to improve is through your reading comprehension. Your level of comprehension might be very good if you are already a skilled reader, but it is an almost inescapable drawback that if you are not careful, your comprehension will go down while speed reading. This can be because of several reasons such as the innate nature of skipping words or sections and the common mistake of moving too fast while reading.

Chapter 6: In-Depth Speed Reading

One way to overcome this is to work on multiple reading processes. You will not really be reading the entire book multiple times with this technique, but you will look at it with varying amounts of depth and with different reasons in mind. Start by previewing what you will be reading with a skimming or scanning technique, then speed read while moving quicker over the material you already understand, then review by writing notes or a summary about what you read. This is a very good tactic for studying.

Another way is to work on your peripheral vision. Since being able to read groups of words is a helpful skill to have while speed reading, making sure you can use your peripheral vision effectively is important. Peripheral vision is the area outside of your usual vision span. There is a narrow point of only about six degrees in which you can easily perceive text with your eyes. By increasing this by just a small amount will have you reading groups of words much easier. Unfortunately, this should not be something you attempt to rely on because the fuzzy part of your vision can be unreliable!

A good way to commit what you read to long-term memory is to imagine debating the author.

Speed Reading

If you actively look for points that counter what the author is presenting, the more emotional your link to what you are reading will be. There is a very strong connection with emotion and reading retention. This is also helpful for learning in a more general sense, outside of reading, because you will naturally become better at recognizing points of interest and arguments as well as form opinions.

If you want to improve your reading comprehension while speed reading, sometimes you only have to look as far as common study advice. It might seem unimportant when learning to speed read, but knowing when to make marks or notes is important to comprehension and can be done even at a sped-up pace. Underlining, circling, highlighting, making short marks or notes in the margin, or even just dog-earing pages will help you remember what you are reading.

Making marks increases your ability to recall the information that you mark. Be careful not to mark too much, however as the marks you make or the pages you save will become less important the more there are. Three to five highlights or underlines per page or about one in ten pages

Chapter 6: In-Depth Speed Reading

can be marked as important enough to come back to.

You should also consider making notes of what you are reading on a separate sheet or transferring important notes or page numbers to the front of the book for easy reference. You might even want to try writing a summary of the book or article when you are done. New information is stored better if it is used within about twenty minutes, meaning if you write something original about it, it will stick longer and easier.

Don't forget to go back, and take note of marked pages especially if you plan to study what you read later. Also, if you can't physically mark the book, like a borrowed or library copy, then use a separate paper and sticky notes.

Another often overlooked way to help you speed read is to simply increase your vocabulary. This happens naturally somewhat but can also be worked on. Someone who knows more words will naturally be better at speed reading as they do not have to stop and look things up or miss out on comprehension due to skipped words. A good way to build your vocabulary is to keep a list of all the words you come across that you do not already know and look them up. Review the list sometimes, and both your vocabulary and speed reading will improve.

Debunking Some Common Speed-Reading Myths:

There is a lot of skepticism out there regarding speed reading so you might be wondering what to say to someone who still doesn't understand how it helps, or maybe you are still skeptical yourself. The common myths and why they are false that are explained below may help boost your confidence in your decision to learn speed reading.

1. Speed reading takes the enjoyment out of much-needed reading. This might be true for a few people, but by-and-large learning how to speed read will help you read more, gain understanding quicker, and teach you how to kick habits that stunt your reading enjoyment.

2. Reading more than 500 words per minute is not possible. This just isn't true. Even average speed readers should be able to pass that mark, and those who are serious

Chapter 6: In-Depth Speed Reading

speed reading learners can reach speeds of over one thousand words per minute. Also, just think of the world record holder of words said per minute (which is undoubtedly more difficult than reading) which is five hundred eighty-six words per minute.

3. You have to use a pacer to speed read. Although a pacer is an indispensable tool in speed reading, you definitely do not have to use one. This is especially true once speed readers get the hang of speed reading. Even if you use one at first, it may become unnecessary as you progress.

4. Reading fast is something only smart people can do. First of all, separating people into "smart" and "not smart" is not a wise thing to do. Also, what we tend to consider "smart" usually boils down to if the person loves to read and is good at it. Therefore, those who learn to speed read may be placed into the "smart" category automatically regardless of other factors.

5. Comprehension is bound to go down when speed reading. Although reading

comprehension may go down if speed reading is done incorrectly and with too much focus on speed alone, truthfully reading fast will increase your concentration and studying capabilities.

6. Words can only be read one at a time. This myth stems from how we are taught to read, where we stop learning new reading techniques after learning to sound out word-by-word what we read. Most people already do or can learn to do at least some clustering while reading, even with minimal work.

7. The results of learning to speed read are temporary. Since reading is a skill, it has to be practiced, or you can lose it. For this reason, this myth is partially true but only if you allow it. Just keeping up with occasional practice once learning to speed read should keep your skills honed.

Choosing When to Speed Read:

One of the most important aspects on your journey towards mastering speed reading is learning when to speed read and when not to speed read. There are positives and negatives to

Chapter 6: In-Depth Speed Reading

speed reading which you should learn and take into account before putting your skills to the test.

Based on your level of practice, concentration, learned skills, whether you are comfortable, and many other variables while reading, a speed reader can reasonably expect to read between five hundred and a few thousand words per minute. At this speed, if you are not careful, you can miss information due to a slip in concentration or misuse of speed reading techniques that will leave you low on comprehension.

A common weakness of speed reading is that it is easy to feel like you understand what you are reading as you go only to forget it a few minutes later. That is why this book has focused so heavily on learning and study skills that you can still use while reading at speeds double, triple, or more of that of an average reader.

If you understand speed reading's limitations, then it should be easy to pick when to use it. When you are reading something for fun, such as a novel or a comic, there is no reason to go out of your way to speed read. You can easily increase how fast you naturally read a novel by learning how to speed read due to increases in things like visualization and vocabulary. but actually speeding through a novel is not something you have to do. Using novels or short stories to practice speed reading is a good way to test comprehension, but for fun speed reading, it is certainly not the norm for speed readers.

If you have time to sit and read something you are trying to learn, such as a textbook or a manual, you should do so. If it is important that you know the details of what you are reading, and you have time to do so, just read it. If you do not have time, combining a multi-reading strategy where you utilize skimming and scanning, speed reading, skipping material you already understand, and reviewing by writing a summary or notes on what you read is very important.

For long reading projects in which you do not have to understand fine details, such as while researching or organizing information, speed reading will be an invaluable tool. You can use any combination of the skills explained in this book to get through as much material and find what you are looking for as quickly as possible.

Chapter 6: In-Depth Speed Reading

This is one of the main reasons for speed reading, and it should be exploited to the fullest.

Your speed reading skills can help you in other aspects of your life that you might not expect. You can get through subtitled films, or television shows quicker, allowing you to keep up with both the dialogue and action on foreign films or if you are hard of hearing. It will be easier to read the text on video games, making your experience easier, especially in games with dialogue or directions flashing on the screen. Driving might become easier if you can process what a sign is saying faster. You will be able to scan an item's label at the store more effectively to find what you need to know. Overall, there are countless times where you can speed read, and you can probably think of even more than are listed here!

Chapter 7:
Advancing Your Speed Reading Skills

Congratulations on making it this far in this book! Hopefully, this means that you have taken a serious interest in speed reading. Honestly, most people who start to learn to speed read will give up, and any practice they put in becomes a waste of their time. As has been mentioned in previous chapters, you cannot give up on your journey to becoming a speed reader. This is likely going to be the single most important piece of advice in this book.

Remember that anyone can learn to speed read, but few can learn to make it useful without some serious effort. You will need to develop good reading habits and practice daily on improving your speed and technique. However, even if after reading this entire book, you do not wish to take on the tasks explained within, hopefully, some of the advice to becoming a better reader will still be helpful for you in the long run.

Speed Reading

On the chance that you wish to become a master speed reader, this chapter will be for you. What this book has taught so far boils down to retraining yourself to read using only visual analysis, and how to make sense of what you read that way. Some people do this naturally, and others have to learn how to do this. Regardless of whether you have a natural talent for speed reading, you can still become quite good at it.

A good way to think of speed reading is that you are presenting a slide show presentation on what you are reading. You take everything you are reading in, organize and decide what is important, and make those parts stick in the long-term memory. This can be visualized like listening to a presenter's speech, taking notes on their slide show, and remembering those key points.

Once you have learned the basics of speed reading, you can make it a habit and do this almost without noticing. You will start to paraphrase everything an author has written automatically. This might make the focus this book puts on active reading make more sense. If a reader is passively accepting the information

Chapter 6: In-Depth Speed Reading

laid out for them, they cannot pick out the key points and retain their comprehension while speed reading.

As a competent speed reader, you will constantly be an active reader and forming a summary of what you read as you go. But once again, be careful and take the advice of the last chapter into consideration to decide when this process is necessary because it is very labor intensive and takes immense focus.

One of the key things a master speed reader will do is master visualization while reading. Although this is a great tool for every reader, speed reading is almost impossible without being able to visualize due to how much slower audio processing is than visual processing in the brain.

If speed reading sounds like something superhuman, well, it kind of is. However, it is still an ability that can be learned and cultivated. The people who perform at the Olympics may be seen as superhuman too, but the difference between them and average people is a lot of work.

Below are several examples of ways to work on building this superhuman ability through techniques just like in previous chapters.

The Mind Map:

Learning to build a mind map is probably one of the best things you can do to improve your visualization skills. A mind map refers to making a diagram to organize information visually in a hierarchical manner displaying relationships between bits of information. Most are built around a central idea which connects the rest of the information to a single point and is usually hand drawn.

The term mind map was popularized by Tony Buzan, a British popular psychology author, but the concept has been around for hundreds of years. This type of visual model system has long been popular for organizing ideas, brainstorming, and problem-solving.

To create a mind map, follow these steps:

1. Start by putting the central idea of what you are reading about in the center of the page.

Chapter 6: In-Depth Speed Reading

2. Select the keywords that are important and connect them with lines to the main idea.

3. Continue connecting ideas, images, and words that radiate out from the central idea.

There are some things to keep in mind while creating your maps. Use multiple colors, codes, and dimensions to show how ideas in what you are reading relate to one another and their importance at a glance. Work on developing a style of mind mapping that is yours so that you can formulate your ideas quickly. Also, be sure to keep things hierarchical and organized.

The SQR3 Method:

This is a technique taught in a lot of college reading courses. SQR3 stands for: Survey, Question, Read, Recite, Review. First, you survey what you are going to read using methods like skimming or scanning. Then you form questions on what the material is saying. After reading while taking notes with those questions in mind, the reader recites their questions and notes. Finally, they review everything they just did.

Speed Reading

This may seem like something that is not compatible with the speed reading process, but that is not the case because speed reading is not about running through the material as fast as you can in one go, but more about efficiency while reading. In most cases, the speed in speed reading is only accomplished by doing a pre-reading process of some kind which helps the reader get into an active reading mindset prior to reading. Speed can be increased even further if you already know what the important points of the text are, or you only want to answer specific questions.

After reading, making sure you understood what you read and committing it to long-term memory is also important, which using this method will ensure. Taking notes and then reviewing them will also help even during times when you do not want to speed read.

Varying Your Speed:

Good speed reading systems should never teach you to only go at one, consistent speed while reading. Doing this makes you more passive as a reader. You need to possess the skill and knowledge of when to slow down and when

Chapter 6: In-Depth Speed Reading

you can speed up to get past less relevant information. This again is a skill that requires being an active reader. Most speed readers vary their speed throughout a section of text to make sure they can understand everything that is written because some reading material automatically will require more thought. Hopefully, this book will give you the skills necessary to put this into practice.

Understanding Reading Comprehension:

To continue improving speed reading techniques, it is just as important to continue improving comprehension. One way to do that is to understand how the human brain can best comprehend what you are reading. There are generally six different types of effective comprehension techniques to try while learning.

The first is *knowing* versus *understanding*. Do you know something from reading it and accepting it as fact, or do you understand it? Strive to really understand what you read. The next is reflecting. Have you made a connection to the information by putting it into your own words? Another type is interpersonal understanding. Check if you understand something by explaining it to someone else. The fourth type is intrapersonal understanding which is finding a way to relate the information that you are reading to your own life. Visualization is another type which is covered extensively in this book. Finally, comprehension is also affected by the difference between mindfulness and acceptance. Are you an active or a passive reader?

These six types of comprehension can work together or separately, and by understanding them, you can better exploit whichever type best works for both you and the type of material you are reading. This can be especially helpful while learning to speed read to be mindful of your level of understanding and alter your practice to accommodate better grasp of the material.

Timing Your Reading Speed and Setting Goals:

Setting goals is a great way to practice and learn new things. For speed reading, a good way to do this is to time your reading speed. You should time yourself before you start learning as a baseline, then as often as you feel is necessary whether that is daily, every few days, or weekly.

Chapter 6: In-Depth Speed Reading

Setting a benchmark and a goal to beat can provide much needed motivation. Of course, do not make speed in words per minute your only goal. Also make goals about breaking habits, learning new skills, and how well you can comprehend while speed reading.

Here is how to time your reading speed. First, you have to find out how many words are on a page. You can either do this by hand or just count one line and multiply that by how many lines are on a page to gain an estimate. Set a timer for ten minutes and see how many pages you can get through in that time. Then multiply the number of pages by the number of words that you made an estimate for. To get the words per minute, just divide by ten.

You can also search for a speed reading application online that will calculate your words per minute for you, however, keep in mind that your speed will likely change when reading digitally compared to reading in print.

After you know your beginning number, you can make a goal. Keep in mind two hundred fifty words per minute is the average of people twelve and older, and about three hundred is the average of most college students. Four hundred and fifty to six hundred words per minute is an average skim rate without speed reading while around one thousand words per minute, you are reaching a master level of speed reading.

To set a realistic and achievable speed reading goal, figure out how fast you want to go. A good average speed to aim for is around six hundred words per minute. You might be faster at times and slower at times. If you are starting with two hundred and fifty words per minute and set a goal for fifty more words per minute, per week, you will take about seven weeks to read that goal.

Making it through this book is a wonderful first step in improving your reading skills and working towards becoming a speed reader. If all has gone well, you now have to tools to read faster and understand more. If nothing else, you should be able to appreciate and enjoy reading more than you did before.

Some last advice for potential speed readers is to enjoy what you are doing and what you are reading! Frustration will kill your aspiration

Chapter 6: In-Depth Speed Reading

faster than anything else. And remember that anyone can be a speed reader including you.

Conclusion

Thank for making it through to the end of *Speed Reading: How to Increase Your Reading Speed, Learning Abilities, and Comprehension*. Let's hope it was informative and able to provide you with all of the tools you need to achieve your goals whatever they may be.

Reading this book will have given you the tools to become a happier, more effective, and faster reader. Hopefully, you have learned how to break any bad reading habits you had, valuable study skills, how to improve visualization and increase reading comprehension, and of course, **how** to read much quicker than you were before.

The next step is to continue practicing and reaching your speed reading goals! Remember that it may take you several weeks, but as long as you do not give up and practice every day, you are sure to become a stronger reader with skills that will last for the rest of your life.

If you enjoyed learning how to speed read using the methods you learned in this book, then be

Speed Reading

sure to tell your friends about the benefits you have received, and how being a faster reader has positively affected your life.

Finally, if you found this book useful in any way, a review on Amazon is always appreciated!

www.ingramcontent.com/pod-product-compliance
Lightning Source LLC
Chambersburg PA
CBHW020529080526
44583CB00013B/795